A Wife's Superpower

*10 Courageous Stories of How to Practice Your
Superpower to Draw the Love You Need from
Your Husband*

Marla,

Thank you for
being a true friend
& helping me get
through this
journey! Love
you dearly!

Faith
Gerner

A Wife's Superpower: 10 Courageous Stories of How to Practice Your Superpower to Draw the Love You Need from Your Husband Copyright © 2018 by Faith G. Joyner. All rights reserved.

Compiled by: Faith G. Joyner, LMFT

Co-Authors: Denise West, Melisha Singh, Teri Stewart, Natasha Redrick, Heather Ross, Keisa Campbell, Colleen Taylor, Earitha Anderson, Tyra Williams

Published by Purple Ribbon Publishing, LLC.

Cover design by Crystal Manu
Content editor Sheila Kennedy
Copy editor Lisa Zahn

ISBN-13: 978-0-9963307-7-0
Printed in the United States of America.
Contact Information: Faith G. Joyner, LMFT
www.faithjoynercounseling.com,
info@faithjoynercounseling.com

Dedication

This book is dedicated to all the wonderful wives across the world.

Table of Contents

Disclaimer

The contents of this book should not be mistaken for appropriate and measured therapy or marriage counseling. If you believe you are a victim of the Three "A's": Abuse, Addiction, or Affairs, then therapeutic advice is necessary but cannot be found in this book. If additional help is necessary beyond identifying your wifely superpower, please see the list of resources located in the back of the book.

The Three "A's"

Although this book is going to completely rock your world (in an awesome way), I want you to keep in mind that it won't and can't address all of the issues every marriage could possibly face. In this book, you're going to find several practical tips that will show you how to assertively, calmly, and confidently operate in your Superpower(s). You may find your Superpower in one chapter or you may find several of your Superpowers throughout this book. That is okay! I'm a firm believer that we have many Superpowers. We've only covered a few.

If you are having problems that are not addressed in this book, I strongly suggest you invest in your marriage and seek marital counseling. If your husband isn't ready for counseling, please don't force him. Believe it or not, seeking individual therapy for yourself could also benefit your marriage. You can learn more about yourself (understanding why you do what you do and feel the way you feel), focus on your role and contribution to whatever is happening in your marriage, and work on ways to change your thoughts and behaviors despite your spouse's lack of motivation to change. When you examine your issues first, it can open the door for your husband to examine his behavior and make it more comfortable for him to have a conversation about your marital issues.

This book is not for wives who are experiencing what counselors call the Three "A's," which are Abuse, Addiction, and Affairs. I counsel domestic violence and sexual abuse survivors, and all of my clients have asked what she could do to make the marriage "better." Every type of abuse is about power and control; it's not about what you've done wrong in the relationship. Being emotionally, verbally, physically, spiritually, or sexually abused is never the victim's fault. Never. You do not deserve this heinous treatment. If you are married to a man who will not stop cheating on you or is struggling with an addiction (drugs, alcohol, gambling, sex, etc.) and will not seek treatment for it, that is not your fault either. Do you hear me?

It will be in your best interest to seek counseling from a therapist who has training in the three "A's" so they can help you navigate through your options while you are on this journey. It is widely suggested by counselors trained in this area that survivors not engage in marriage or couples therapy with an abuser. Marriage therapy is about both partners taking responsibility for their actions and putting forth an effort to change the behaviors that are causing the issues in their relationship. Abusers don't take responsibility for their actions and even if they do they try to minimize it in a way that still blames the person being abused. You can attend counseling on your own and your abusive spouse needs to attend counseling on his own (including a program specifically for abusive partners). There are also support groups you can attend if you are the spouse of an addict (including sexual addiction). If you are experiencing the three "A's," please refer to my additional resources page at the end of this book to find out where you can start to receive help.

~ Faith G. Joyner, LMFT

Introduction

Wifely Superpowers are the unique skills and personal strengths a wife innately possesses that give her the ability to experience her husband's heart like no one else does. These skills and strengths create safety, support, accountability, and trust in a way that will and can transform a marriage.

When we operate in our Superpowers, our husbands value our input and are naturally and consistently drawn to us to fulfill our needs. This is NOT manipulation or control, but positive influence and energy used for the good of the marriage. Neither is this being a doormat or not having a voice in your marriage. In this book, my co-authors and I are going to show you how to assertively and confidently use your Superpowers in ways that do not cause intimidation or confusion in your marriage. When you learn how to use your Superpowers, you will be equipped to take on marriage issues in a different way…with patience and wisdom.

Of course, your husband is still going to aggravate the hell out of you sometimes, but hey, that's just the nature of being married. While you're laughing about him aggravating you so much, please understand that you aggravate him sometimes too. Again, just the nature of being married. Sometimes we're going to annoy each other, but that doesn't mean we don't love each other.

I want you to take pride in the ability to see and know your husband's heart like no one else can. It is special. It is intimate. For me, I know there's a way that, when I use my Superpower of Communication, it makes my husband Jamahl blush so cutely. No one else has that effect on him. Jamahl has come to trust my Superpower and believe in it in such a way that he asks for my opinions and actually listens to me!

"Faith, why do I have to operate in this Superpower? Why can't he?" Well, women hold the most influence in the relationship, my dear. We set the tone in the marriage and our household. You know that adage, *"Happy wife, happy life,"* right? Research has shown that it's actually true. A study of 394 couples revealed that the wife's satisfaction played a huge role in the happiness or misery of the marriage[1]. The study also revealed that how the wives felt about

the marriage was a factor in whether or not the husband was happy or not in the marriage[1]. Please do not use this as an excuse to be controlling, manipulative, mean, or nasty. Ultimately, if you act this way you will not have a happy husband or marriage, and if you keep acting this way you may not have a husband. Just use this as an example to show that we carry powerful influence and must learn to use it right.

The study showed that if the husband is miserable, then the marriage suffers less[1]. This does not mean that we're better, superior, or smarter than our husbands. We know that's not true. This just means that women carry most of the influence from the beginning of the relationship all the way into marriage. I've also discovered in my own marriage that when I focused on myself first and stopped pointing the finger (although this brother was equally wrong and had issues), Jamahl was more open to focusing on himself and making some changes within himself. I discovered on my healing journey that my past affected my present, how I viewed myself, and how I viewed my husband. And guess what? Jamahl has a past too, which affected the way he viewed himself and the way he viewed me. We gave each other time and space to grow. Being a survivor of sexual abuse and ending my unhealthy first marriage, I went through my own healing process and learned that the abuse wasn't my fault, learned how to rewrite my narratives, discovered how to transform my life to get positive results, and learned how to use my Superpowers to not only improve my marriage but to help my husband understand how I needed to be loved. And oh, is he loving him some Faith!

So, what is your Superpower? What do you do that only you can do for your husband that brings safety, support, trust, and accountability to your marriage? What do you do that brings relief to him? What do you do that guides and protects him from harm? What do you do that makes him feel like he has the best woman in the world? I'm not talking about sex either. Superpowers are deeper than being able to make love to your husband. They're skills that enable you to bring the best out of your husband so that you can receive the best from him.

Want your husband to be more attentive to you? I'm going to answer this question in the nicest way I can so please hear my heart in this. If you want your husband to be more attentive to you, then you have to get a life. What do I mean by this? Well, I've learned from professional and personal experience that when we as wives take care of ourselves by having and participating in our own interests and hobbies, taking the time to hang out with our friends, pursuing our dreams, and setting limits on what we do or don't do in relationships (such as saying "no" or not being coerced to participate in activities we don't want to participate in), husbands are attracted to that and want to get to know us better. They want to know where we're going. They want to know how long we have been interested. They want to know what the benefits are from doing all these wonderful things we're doing. It's not out of control, but they are genuinely interested in us. Let me give you two examples of how this looks.

First, I once counseled a wife who had been married for over 20 years. We'll call her Susan for confidentiality reasons. Susan believed she had outgrown her husband and marriage. She was miserable. She could not stand her husband! Susan's husband was nice to her, but there was no passion or intimacy in their marriage. Everything was routine and stagnant.

He wasn't financially responsible, but she was responsible for the household chores, paying the bills, and resolving everyone's issues in their family (on both sides). Susan had lost herself in her marriage and in being a mother. She knew that at this stage of her life she needed to stop focusing on him. She came into counseling only wanting to focus on herself and her growth as a woman. I asked her, *"Who are you?"* and she broke down crying. After 20 years of marriage, three children, several relocations and job opportunities, and being over 40, she had no clue on how to answer that question.

I asked her, *"What did you like to do before you got married?"* Susan answered, *"I used to love to dance. I used to go out dancing all the time. I had so much fun. It made me laugh and it gave me energy."* I then asked, *"What's stopping you from doing that now?"* Susan replied, *"Time, being married, having children, being in ministry, the list goes on. I can't focus on that now because I have other things to focus on. Plus, I really want my husband to go out dancing with me, but he won't do it."* I gave her a homework assignment. Her homework assignment was to find a reputable place where she could go dancing by herself or with some friends. She was to make sure that she respected the common courtesy of her marriage to not come home too late (whatever too late meant for their marriage) and to make sure that she informed her husband of where she was going and how long she was going to be out. Well, she did the assignment and loved it!

She and some close friends dressed up and prepared for a night of dancing. As she was walking out the door, her husband noticed her and asked, "*Where are you going?*" Susan gently responded, "*I told you last week that I was going out with Lisa to go dancing. We're going to 'such and such' and I'll be home by 1:30am.*" She said that was the first time in years he had asked her where she was going. She kept up with this homework assignment for three months before her husband decided to come along with her. Susan shared that he looked at her in ways he hadn't in a long time. They had a great time together, and it was the beginning of a rejuvenated marriage. Since Susan was focusing on herself and her growth, she had less time to focus on her husband and how he wasn't making her happy.

Secondly, I personally had a huge people-pleasing problem and would accept invites for events or let people talk me into things I didn't want to do. Jamahl would always ask, *"Well, if you don't want to do it, then why are you doing it? Why are you going? Why are you talking to her?"* I could tell he was irritated and confused about this behavior. Later, in one of our intimate conversations he revealed to me that my people-pleasing behavior sowed seeds of mistrust in him about me. If I couldn't really stand up for myself and was being fake about where I wanted to spend my time and energy, he couldn't really trust my words to him. He couldn't really trust that when I said "yes" to him, it was coming from a genuine place. When I changed my people-pleasing behavior, Jamahl became more attentive to me. He listened to me more. He became more patient towards me. He wanted to know more about my dreams of helping wives. He knew that he could trust me. I learned that taking care of myself and letting my "no" be and mean "no" strengthened my personal boundaries and my connection with my husband.

See, we've been taught, whether directly or indirectly, that doing everything for our husbands and focusing on them and the children will make us happy. We've been taught that our role is to "stay on top of things" so everyone's worlds won't crash under them. We've been taught that depending on our husbands to make us happy will make us happy. We've been taught that focusing on our husbands and micromanaging their flaws and weaknesses will make our husbands magically come to their senses and say, *"You know what? All of my wife's nagging has been spot on! I've been such a fool. I need to change today!"* Nope, that's not how this works. That's not how any of this works. We fear that if we get a life we will lose our husband to someone else. We've been misguided to believe that being Superwoman will keep a man, and that's just not true.

I've counseled several wives who were like Susan, and their husbands still cheated on them or left them to be with someone else. Honey, if your man wants to cheat or leave it's because he wants to cheat or leave; it's not because you're not being Superwoman. How is this Superwoman complex (we talk about that more later on in this introduction) working out for you? How has taking care of everyone else and neglecting yourself improved your marriage and strengthened you as a woman? My guess is that it hasn't benefited you at all. I know it didn't benefit me. Moreover, sometimes we put so much of the focus on our husbands and how wrong they are, or how they're not making us happy, all in an attempt to not focus on our own mess. It's more comfortable focusing on someone else's faults.

That way, we think, it takes the focus off of our faults. No matter how much you try to place the blame on him, there's a lot you've done to contribute to the breakdown of your marriage, including not speaking up for yourself.

So, what's the lesson? Stop it! Just stop it! Get a life! Discover who you are as a woman. What did you like doing before marriage and children? What were you or are you passionate about? If money wasn't an issue, what would you be doing now for a living or a hobby? Take the dance class by yourself. Go to the movies by yourself. Go to your favorite restaurant by yourself. Get your hair styled. Buy that outfit. Get those shoes. Go back to school. Get that certificate. Eat the damn cookie! Whatever makes you feel like yourself and makes you smile, do it. You'll discover that getting a life has more benefits than you could have ever imagined. It's okay to have a life outside of your marriage. It does not mean you have to neglect your husband, children, or your responsibilities either. You can have your own life and still stay connected to your husband. You're more than just your husband's wife. Remember that.

Let me tell you what this book is NOT about. It's not about you being Superwoman. Because you're not her. This book isn't about you being all things, to all people, at all times. That's unrealistic and unhealthy. There was a study conducted in 2010 by Dr. Cheryl L. Woods-Giscombe[2] and she researched how the Superwoman complex affects women; specifically, African American women and their views on stress, strength, and health.

The idea of Superwoman was partially developed in reaction to African American women trying to combat the negative stereotypes of African American women, such as:

- Welfare Queen: The black woman who is lazy and continues to have children with no paternal support and is dependent on the government for financial means.
- Jezebel: The black woman who is innately promiscuous, lacks self-respect, and uses her body as a sexual weapon.

- Mammy: The black maternal figure who cared for her white family and was content being a slave.

The Superwoman contribution of "being strong and just dealing with it" highlights hidden attributes that African American women have had to endure despite racism, adversity, and oppression.[2]

The study included eight focus groups of African American women and they discovered these five characteristics of having to obtain the Superwoman complex: the obligation to show strength, the obligation to suppress emotions, the resistance to being vulnerable or dependent, the determination to succeed despite limited resources, and the obligation to help others.[2] Ma'am, whether you're Black, White, Hispanic, Asian, Native American, or Bi-Racial, I am not telling you to take on these characteristics. The study participants reported that all of these characteristics led to relationship strain. Not being able to be vulnerable prevented them from being loved or loving others fully or dominating relationships in fear of being vulnerable. Secondly, it led to stress-related emotional health issues such as emotional eating, no self-care activities, smoking, dysfunctional sleeping patterns, depression, etc. Lastly, it led to stress-related physical health issues such as weight gain/loss, panic attacks, hair loss, migraines, etc.[2] All of that is unnecessary. I am not telling you to be Superwoman and set yourself on fire to keep others warm. To the contrary, you will see how the other authors and myself have strongly suggested that you take care of yourself first before you take care of anyone else. Before you focus on your husband, focus on yourself. You cannot pour from an empty cup. When you take care of yourself first, you are better equipped to care for your husband and children.

Finally, as you read this book and discover some of your Superpowers, contemplate your needs and how you desire to get those needs met. Consider how you want to use your voice to impact your marriage. It is important for you to remember that you even have a voice. My hope is that you discover how to use your voice and your influence for good. For the good of your own life and your marriage.

~ Faith G. Joyner, LMFT

Chapter 1:
Communication

Faith G. Joyner, LMFT

"How many times do we have to have this conversation?"

This is what I'm thinking, but don't say aloud to my husband when I've had to explain something to him more than once.

"As smart and intelligent as you are, can't you spit out how you're feeling when I ask? We're having this important conversation about our relationship and the best reply you can give is…I don't know?"

*"Oh, but when it's something **you** want to do or talk about, you're all into that conversation, huh? You have a Plan A, Plan B, and a Plan C, right?"* Yes, I'm having a whole conversation within myself trying not to interrupt the flow of a productive conversation with my husband, Jamahl.

Anyone who knows me, knows that I love me some Jamahl. I think the world of him and am grateful for who he is in my life. I honestly believe he is *The One* for me. This man is wise beyond his years, and I benefit from his sage advice on a daily basis. He's my best friend, lover, and protector. I am safe with him. I can't imagine my life without him; neither do I want to imagine it. However, sometimes he really annoys me when it comes to his communication style! After 14 years, I'm less annoyed, because he's come a long way from years past. We've grown to understand each other's communication styles and have learned to adjust when needed. One of the lessons I've learned in my 14-year marriage is to think before I speak. That is why I pause before saying the immediate things that come to mind, which would neither be productive nor accomplish anything positive in that moment. It will only shut him down and prevent him from opening up when it really does matter.

Earlier in my marriage, I was manipulative and controlling. I would pout when I didn't get my way. I would speak over Jamahl to *outtalk* him. Ooooh! I was so nice-nasty (in the counseling field this is called passive-aggressive). *"I'm just trying to be the submissive wife, so I don't have anything to say since I'm not supposed to have an opinion anyway,"* I said with a smile and a sarcastic tone. I would try to make him feel inferior because he couldn't think as fast as I could think in the heat of the moment during an argument. "*So, since I'm **always** trying to tell you how to spend the money, tell me the last time I did it? Oh, you can't think of it now? But... I do it all the time, so you should have at least one example to give me.*" I used my gift of speaking and communicating to try to get what I wanted from Jamahl. Of course, this did not work all of the time. Jamahl would become infuriated, yell or shut down, and do the opposite of what I was asking at the time. Unfortunately, this was a vicious cycle in my marriage. I came from a family who used shouting and badgering to get their way. Jamahl came from a family who used fear and intimidation tactics to get their way; both of us had a lot of growing up to do.

A concept about communication that some people are not aware of is that it is not only about *giving* information, but it is also about *receiving* information. Merriam-Webster defines communication[3] as a process by which information is *exchanged* between individuals through a common system of symbols, signs, or behaviors. When people are communicating with each other, they need to give each other fair and equal attention and time to speak. This was not happening in my marriage. It was difficult for me to look at myself in the mirror and realize I was not being fair to my husband. He deserved time to think about what he needed and how to articulate that to me. Jamahl wouldn't think or speak fast enough for me, so I was rude and disrespectful to him. Wives and wives-to-be (if you desire to be a wife one day, you're a wife-to-be), this is called *control*.

I realized I needed to change when I found out Jamahl made purchases of large amounts without letting me know; he kept it a secret for a long time. Jamahl has expensive tastes and likes what he likes. I was controlling and didn't want him to spend what I thought was too much money. Now, he wasn't misusing our household finances; rent was paid; all the bills were paid; credit card debt was going down; and the savings account was growing. We were able to go on dates with each other and outings with our friends. I was able to get my get my hair styled and he was able to get his hair cut on a regular basis. In reality, I was overreacting and it wasn't that serious. Jamahl didn't believe I would approve of him getting some leisure gifts for himself, because I was always nagging about money and saving.

A Wife's Superpower

I had a huge fear of being broke. First of all, who am I to not approve a grown man treating himself after all of his responsibilities are taken care of? Jamahl has never been neglectful in taking care of us, so what was the problem? It was me. I wasn't being fair. I wasn't letting him communicate his needs to me. When I found out he made those purchases, I was hurt and surprised. We talked about everything, or so I thought. I asked him why he didn't tell me about the purchases and he replied, "*I don't know.*" I suspected it was because I was being irrational and too hard on him about our finances. I did not give him an opportunity to use his voice when it came to that topic.

Throughout my time as a marriage counselor and learning from my own marriage, I've discovered that couples believe they have a *communication problem* as the reason they are coming in for counseling. It's not a communication problem; it's a maturity problem. Couples are not mature enough to hear that their partner has a different opinion, conviction, political view, or worldview from them, and it irritates them to no end. They get caught up in the cycle of trying to get their partner to think the way they think, or to get on their side. Again, this is called *control*. This was my problem (and Jamahl's problem, but we're not talking about him and his issues right now). When I stopped trying to control Jamahl and operated using my Superpower of Communication, I saw new and healthy behaviors in my husband. He openly communicated more about his thoughts and feelings, and he stopped hiding things from me and discontinued the silent treatment behavior he gave me for a long time in our marriage.

I want to share one of the ways I stopped trying to control Jamahl. I practice this even today in our marriage, and it works brilliantly. If we're arguing (not yelling but having a heated discussion) and Jamahl needs time to think about what he wants and how he feels, I give my husband time to think about how he feels, what he believes, and how he wants to communicate that to me. This time may be one to two days.

You might be thinking, *"One to two days, Faith? Ain't nobody got time for that!"* On the contrary my friend, yes, you do. See, I have come into the knowledge that Jamahl did not grow up talking about feelings, communicating his beliefs, or having someone close to him really listen to his needs. Because of this, it may take him a longer time to formulate the words he's comfortable with in order to communicate to me when I ask him, *"How do you feel about this?"* Or, *"What should we do?"*

My man is a thinker and a fixer. Remember, I said earlier that he's wise. I've learned to give him time to operate in his gifts. This takes patience that I've had time to practice over the years. If I force him to give me an answer he doesn't have or doesn't know how to articulate to me in the moment, that's not going to accomplish anything. It's only going to tick the both of us off and delay a resolution. He is not a little boy. He is not my son. He doesn't have to give me an answer when and how I want him to give me an answer. I am not his mother. I'm his wife who wants to resolve this issue as peacefully as we can. Is this annoying sometimes? Hell yeah! But it gets easier with time and practice.

I used to be afraid to give him this much time. I would think, *"What if he doesn't really think about it?"* or *"What if he really doesn't care?"* My husband loves me and wants to make our marriage great just like I do. Even if I have to remind him we need to talk, it's okay, because that's my strength not his. It does not mean he doesn't care. There are several things Jamahl has to remind me of that matter to him. It does not mean that I don't care; I just forgot. We exchange strengths for weaknesses.

So how does this look in our marriage today? We're in a deep conversation. Both of us are irritated. I ask him, "*Well, what do you want to do?*" and he replies, "*I'm not sure yet.*" Now, I'm angry. Of course, I'm thinking, "*I know what I want to do, why don't you? Is it that difficult to come to a conclusion right now? I want to get this over with now!*" I don't say what I'm thinking. I clasp my hands together, take a deep breath, and ask, "*Can we come back to this in a day or two, so we can conclude this discussion?*" He responds with frustration in his tone, "*Yeah.*" We move on with our lives. We still speak to each other (no silent treatment). Once a day or two has passed, I remind him of our conversation and then he pours out his heart to me. I get to hear things I probably wouldn't have heard if I didn't give him time to process. He helps me understand him in ways I didn't before, and he communicates to me that he's willing to do whatever he needs to do to resolve this issue. We come up with a game plan, compromise if we need to, and resolve that problem. Our relationship then goes to higher level of compassion, peace, and intimacy.

Here are some other lessons I've learned throughout my marriage about effective and productive communication. First, I don't take on Jamahl's emotions. Just because he's in a foul mood doesn't mean I have to be. I practice letting him have his own emotions by leaving the room (to focus on positive energy); hanging up the phone (I don't hang up without letting him know I'm hanging up); or requesting to discuss matters later (when we are both calm). I remember he's grown and can have whatever feelings he wants to have. By the same token, I'm also grown and don't have to subject myself to his salty mood, attitude, or behavior. I give him time and space to settle his nerves and continue to live my BEST life. I stopped taking things so personally. I used to take things personally due to my history of abuse, which led to low self-esteem. Everything is not about me. His attitude and behavior isn't always about what I'm doing wrong. They're about him having a bad attitude.

Next, I stopped trying to get him to understand ideas he just didn't understand. It became nagging at that point. Understanding is important in a marriage, but it isn't a prerequisite to actions or follow through. I stopped waiting on Jamahl to *understand* what I need all the time. He doesn't have to understand; he just needs to be my husband and partner and come through for me. Jamahl and I don't understand each other's needs all the time, but our love for each other supersedes understanding. As long as I'm asking for something reasonable, then *understanding* isn't necessary.

I have counseled several wives who have explained themselves over and over to their husbands about needing time away from the house or needing help with household chores or something else really important to them, and their husbands just *don't understand*. So these wives continue to be miserable because they believe that in order to take action, they need the understanding of their husbands first. No, ma'am, that's not true. Your life cannot stop, nor must it be dreadful because your husband doesn't understand every need you have. Be respectful, responsible, and accountable to your husband but also take care of yourself, express your boundaries, and do what's best for you. He needs to be considerate and fulfill your reasonable needs because he simply loves you.

Lastly, I am consistent and follow through on my expressed boundaries. This means, when I set a boundary with Jamahl and say, "*I'm not going to engage with you when you're speaking to me in a rude tone,*" I walk away from the conversation and do not speak to him if he's being rude to me. I don't egg on the conversation. I don't try to get him to understand why I believe he's being rude. I let him know I'm about to walk away, and then I walk away until both of us can speak to each other in a calm manner. Yes! This works! He knows he isn't going to get a response from me and there won't be a resolution to our issues if he continues to speak to me in that way.

**Here are three practical ways to use
Communication to naturally and consistently
draw the love you need from your husband:**

1. **Shed your arrogance**. Your thoughts and
   ways are not superior to your husband's
   thoughts and ways. You are not God. You are
   not All-Knowing. Just because your husband
   thinks differently doesn't mean he's wrong. If
   you present yourself as superior to him, then
   he *feels* that energy from you and will lose his
   sense of safety in your presence when it
   comes to expressing his thoughts and
   feelings. Your husband's differences should
   not feel like a threat to your existence. If they
   do, then that's something you need to work
   on for yourself. Compromise by
   acknowledging his strengths first and then
   express your thoughts about the situation.
   This will take you further than you can ever
   imagine.

2. **If time is needed to process feelings, ideas,
   and resolutions, give it to him or let him
   know you need it.** If he tries to pressure you
   to talk when you don't want to talk, say
   something like this, *"I know that this is an
   important matter for both of us, and I want to*

resolve this as much as you do. I need time to process my thoughts and feelings, so can we agree to come together tomorrow to finish this conversation?" You are a grown woman, not a little girl, and do not have to be pressured into anything. Use this technique wisely; don't use it as an excuse to not resolve issues.

3. **Develop self-control.** The only person you can control in this marriage is yourself. Focus on yourself for the next 30 days. Don't focus on your husband and what he's not doing or how different he is from you. Whatever you need to work on, work on it via online video courses, books, individual counseling, group counseling, or personal development seminars/workshops/conferences. Your attitude about yourself and your marriage will change drastically.

Personal Notes About Communication

_____

_____

_____

_____

_____

_____

_____

_____

_____

_____

_____

_____

_____

_____

_____

_____

_____

_____

_____

_____

_____

_____

_____

_____

_____

About Faith Joyner, LMFT

Faith loves to see people thrive and reach their full potential. Her passion for people began early in her career when she served in the United States Air Force. While in the Air Force, she traveled to several countries, including Germany where she met her wonderful husband of 14 years, Jamahl.

Since then, she has received her Bachelor's degree in Psychology and her Master's degree in Marriage and Family Therapy and her passion grew even stronger. Faith has over nine years of experience working with individuals, couples, and families. Her clients have described her as honest, trustworthy, and compassionate. Faith uses her professional and personal experience to help people develop and cultivate healthy relationships. She accomplishes this by conducting relationship counseling and coaching, speaking at marriage conferences, and hosting her own *For Wives Only* Workshops. She is also an author of the marriage-themed book, *Your Tool Guide for a Happy Marriage: Practical Solutions on How to Build a Thriving Marriage*.

Faith is a Licensed Marriage & Family Therapist in the state of Florida. She is currently working towards her licensure in the state of Georgia. Faith is also a PhD student studying Trauma and Disaster Relief due to her service as an advocate for survivors of domestic and sexual trauma.

Faith loves chocolate, traveling, and suspense movies. Lastly, she enjoys spending quality time with her husband and friends. You can reach her at info@faithjoynercounseling.com and on Facebook and Instagram at @forwivesonly.

Acknowledgments

First, I want to thank God for the courage to pursue my dreams and be true to myself. It is not easy; my strength comes from HIM.

A Wife's Superpower

To my beautiful husband, Jamahl, who never requires me to dim my light. I love you, Boo. To my FamFriends (friends who became my family) who supported, encouraged, and spoke life to me throughout this process.

Last but not least, I truly admire my co-authors and their gifts. Thank you for allowing me to be on this journey with you. I love you all. We did it!

Chapter 2:
Introspection

Denise West

Merriam-Webster defines *introspection*[4] as a reflective looking inward: an examination of one's own thoughts and feelings. It sounds so simple and to some extent, it is. Everyone has the ability to look within, to reflect, and to examine their thoughts and feelings. The difference though, is what you do with what you find. The choices you make can move you forward or leave you stagnant. If I think back far enough, I've been unconsciously introspective since I was a preteen, but over the years it has been more intentional. It has brought tremendous change and growth in my life.

Introspection: Reflection + Choices = Change

The first five years of marriage introduced me to the choices and challenges that come with a life-long relationship. After about a year of building our friendship and getting to know each other, Ron and I realized we wanted to spend our lives together. Unlike most couples, we got married before we had our wedding. We wanted a wedding but needed time to save the money to pay for it. So, one day after church we were married by our pastor in front of two close friends and only our parents knew about it. Oddly enough, my first foray into the challenges of married life would start with planning my wedding.

I had lived on my own for a few years, plus I was (and am) fiercely independent and incredibly strong-willed. I was accustomed to making decisions without consulting or considering anyone else. People had told me that guys didn't really care about wedding plans, so I was fully prepared to create the wedding I wanted, with no input from Ron or anyone else.

My first task was choosing the colors. Imagine my surprise when Ron asked to see what I had chosen. My reaction was one of indignation: "Why would he want to see my colors?" So he said to me, "I don't want to look at wedding pictures years from now and see colors I don't like." I thought, *What? Why would you not like the colors I picked? I have great taste and it doesn't matter what you think.* I really wanted him to let me do this by myself; of course, to my dismay, Ron wanted to be involved in everything.

My initial reaction was to push back; weddings were about the bride and I should get to do what I wanted, and he should let me. Then I thought about it (*reflection*): I was not the only one getting married, it was his wedding too. Did I want to spend time arguing and did I really want to push him out of this if he wanted to be included? Was I being selfish and controlling? This was going to be a big thing for us, so why shouldn't we do it together? I chose to treat my marriage like the partnership it was, and my husband and I planned our wedding together. I discovered that I liked doing things with Ron and he lowered my stress levels; plus, he had good ideas and we worked well together.

Over the next few years, I did a lot of reflecting, making choices, and changing on all sorts of things; including how to manage our finances, volunteering together, where to spend holidays, and buying a house. My husband was more motivated to compromise and change when he saw me working on myself to make our marriage work for both of us.

Introspection: Reflection + Choices = Change

A Wife's Superpower

The next five years of our marriage presented some major difficulties for us. We ventured into unfamiliar territory and almost didn't make it to year ten. Things in our marriage were going really well. We had adjusted to sharing the same space and making decisions together. Then we got pregnant, and the next phases of stress were about to begin. What I am about to tell you I share with you in retrospect, but at the time, I had no awareness of my mental and emotional state.

Being pregnant can wreak havoc on the hormones of a woman and cause temporary emotional and behavioral changes. In my case, it felt like my mind and emotions went haywire permanently. It started when we found out we were having a little girl. I thought, *How am I going to protect a little girl? I have to protect her.* Something inside me snapped. I found myself on the defense against my husband, yet he was not on offense or defense against me. It was like an out of body experience. I listened to myself snap at him. I wanted to stop, but the harsh words kept coming. I watched myself criticize him and the emotions were uncontrollable. My logical brain knew Ron was doing everything he could and should be doing. The reflective part of me noted that Ron was loving and caring. He was very accommodating;

he would even drive across town to get milkshakes for me in the middle of the night. Sometimes, the results of our reflection get ignored. Despite what I knew and felt in my heart, I never told him I appreciated him, and I barely thanked him for anything. I had changed, this time for the worst. Ron was a trooper. He was looking forward to the baby coming and there were times when things were good between us. He chalked up my unpredictable behavior and erratic emotions to the pregnancy and toughed it out. After the baby was born, I did not go back to normal. I became depressed, but I had no idea what was happening.

Sometimes, *reflection* will sneak up on you. I had convinced myself that things were fine. I was in control and taking care of my daughter. I had a new job and Ron was doing his thing. We were running a household together, and our child was thriving and happy. Our marriage, however, was not thriving or happy. We were coexisting like roommates raising a child together. I had convinced myself that this was working, that other people lived like this for years and they were content, so we could be too. One night, I had settled in bed for the night and Ron lay down beside me to talk. Talking was not something we

22

did unless it was to get things done for the house or our daughter. He told me he was unhappy and was leaving. He told me it didn't seem like I wanted to be with him, because we were hardly ever intimate, and I was not really talking to him anymore. He told me I rejected him and seemed to have no respect for him.

What was I hearing? I lay there in tears and listened to every word. I went into quiet thought about what he was saying, deep reflection and apprehension that my marriage could be ending. I could have become defensive and put the blame on him, but I had to see the truth, do the difficult thing, and look at myself with a critical eye. Everything he said was true, I had shut him out and pushed him away by being distant. I chose to tell my husband that I wanted him to stay. I apologized to him, and then the real work began. Choosing to battle your own demons is one of the most difficult things in the world, but when you come out on the other side a stronger and better you, it's worth it.

Introspection: Reflection + Choices = Change

The next five years of marriage pushed me into new waters. Ron was offered a great job that required us to move to a new city. This relocation meant I would have to leave my job, my friends, and my family behind and move to a place where everything and everyone would be new to me. I had never been in this situation; I had always moved to places where I knew at least one person who was able to introduce me to others.

This was a good time to make a move though. Our daughter was getting ready to start kindergarten, so she was already going to be transitioning to a new school with new kids and new teachers. On the other hand, I had just worked my way out of a serious depression and the move could be a setback. However, it was a major career move for Ron plus a big financial boost for our family, and I wanted to support my husband, so we moved.

For the first six months after the move, I decided not to work. I kept busy making the transition to a new house and getting our daughter set for school. Ron was busy settling into his new job and making work friends. I became lonely. I was volunteering at my daughter's school and going to activities with ladies from the new church we were attending, but I couldn't seem to make friends. I missed my friends and felt depressed. I cried when I was alone. I had never had difficulty making friends in my life and I just couldn't figure out what was happening. I had lots of time to think and reflect on what was happening, but it simply made no sense that I wasn't making friends. I have never been shy a day in my life and dang it, people like me.

I believe all things happen for a reason, so what was this about? I thought a lot about where Ron and I were in our relationship. We were doing better since the depression and the tough times when I had been so distant, but we still weren't where we had been earlier in our relationship. I realized this could be an opportune time to rebuild my friendship with my husband, so I stopped trying to find friends and let myself get back to enjoying my husband's company. Ron and I focused on getting reacquainted; we started dating and going places without our daughter. We discovered what was missing, and our relationship improved. Without trying, I started making friends again, but my husband became my best friend—the way it should have been all along.

Introspection: Reflection + Choices = Change

The last five years of marriage have been a time of growth. For fifteen years, Ron and I repeatedly dealt with certain areas of difficulty. We would work out an issue, things would go well for a time, and then after a while we would be having the same argument. Our regular issues were communication and intimacy. Remember, I told you I was strong-willed and accustomed to being in control. Over the years, I would forget that my husband was my partner and not someone to be managed. I would tell him things to do and instruct him as though he was incapable of doing things "right." This was a regular point of contention for us, with him reminding me that he was not my child. After many years of correcting this, I had to take a good hard look at myself and reflect on why I kept doing this to Ron.

I have always thought he was one of the smartest people I know. He was quite capable of doing things, and I knew that. Why did things have to be done my way and on my schedule? I recognized this was all about control. I challenged myself to talk with my husband and not at him. I made a decision to listen with intention. I made the effort to be honest, really honest. My honesty could be true, but not hurtful. I shared all of this with Ron and he decided to do the same. This has been so freeing for us. My husband and I have talked about things that we walked on eggshells about for years. Committing to truly open communication has been one of the best relationship decisions I've ever made.

Introspection: Reflection + Choices = Change

The intimacy issue was complex. When it came to discussing intimacy, I discovered Ron was not fully honest about his feelings because he didn't want to seem like a jerk. I would get defensive when he brought up the issue of the lack of intimacy. We were intimate, but not as often as he would have liked and not as often as we had been in the past. I loved my husband and wanted all aspects of our relationship to thrive. So, I reflected on the years of our marriage and had to face a sad reality: I had a problem with intimacy and I knew why. When I was a child I was molested, and it negatively affected me in many ways, especially in intimacy with my husband. This was why I put up my defenses to protect my daughter from a danger that didn't exist in my home. I wanted to believe I had put that demon behind me, but it would not stay away. I had to accept that I couldn't fix it alone, so, for the first time in my life, I went to see a licensed mental health counselor. It was a very positive and eye-opening experience. The counselor helped me in ways I would have never been able to do on my own. Ron was motivated to see a counselor too. We have strengthened our marriage and learned what it takes to make continuous improvements in our relationship.

I have been married for over 20 years now. Being introspective has gotten me through difficult times throughout my marriage, and it has helped me to grow as a person and as a wife. Consistent reflection has presented me with many choices that have brought positive change to my husband and me. Ron has watched me make choices and changes and because of that, he made his own personal changes. Being introspective has required me to tread some unfamiliar waters, step into unknown territory, and challenge myself, but it has made my life so rich.

Introspection: Reflection + Choices = Change

Here are three practical ways to use Introspection to naturally and consistently draw the love you need from your husband:

1. **Be brave enough to look at yourself with a critical eye when issues arise in your marriage.** Think about how the issue developed and look at your part in it. Consider your choices for moving forward and determine which choices might lead to positive changes.

2. **Be strong enough to reflect on your own responses and reactions.** Pay attention to your husband's demeanor after your interactions and conversations with him. Ask yourself if your tone of voice, words, and actions are sending messages of love, respect, and support or intolerance, disdain, and obstruction. Consider how you might interact with your husband in a way that will be effective and uplifting for both of you.

3. **Be mature enough to choose to change when you see room for improvement.** For as awesome as we are, we always have room for improvement. What are those recurring issues in

your marriage? Ask yourself why an issue keeps coming up. Look at your choices for making change. Do you do well following tips from books? Should you consult a counselor? Do you have wise and honest friends who will help you change and hold you accountable?

Personal Notes About Introspection

_____

_____

_____

_____

_____

_____

_____

_____

_____

_____

_____

_____

_____

_____

_____

_____

_____

_____

_____

_____

_____

_____

_____

_____

About Denise West

Denise West is a native of Mississippi and a current resident of Florida. She discovered during college that she has the gift of gab, so she honed her focus by earning a Bachelor's degree in Mass Communications from Jackson State University and went on to earn a Master's degree in Public Relations from Michigan State University. Denise has been married to her husband, Ron, for over 20 years and they have a daughter in college. Through an honest and caring approach, Denise and Ron share marriage tips and pitfalls with other couples by hosting a website and podcast called 20-to-Life Marriage (www.20tolifemarriage.com).

Denise enjoys sharing with others and has an affinity towards the importance of communicating with your spouse. She is currently an accreditation administrator in graduate medical education for a major university. Denise can be contacted via email at twentytolifemarriage@icloud.com, and you can follow her on Instagram at denisewest5056 and Twitter at dtesheila.

Acknowledgements

I would like to:

Thank God for creating the connections to allow me to share my experiences with others. Without Him I would be nothing.

Acknowledge my awesome husband, Ron, for loving me and always being supportive and encouraging, no matter what my endeavors.

Thank Faith Joyner for trusting me to be a part of this project and seeing something in me that I initially couldn't see in myself.

A special thank you to my daughter, Sydni, my parents, and my inner circle, the "Abnormals" (you know who you are). You all inspire me to be the best me that I can be, simply because you love me.

Chapter 3:
Vulnerability

Melisha Singh

VULNERABILITY

Vulnerability[5] is defined as:

Your "ability" to be vulnerable.

Your deep expression of your most sacred thoughts and feelings.

Willingness to share yourself with others authentically and without apology.

Exposing your flaws, secrets, and darker sides without shame.

(Taken from: *How to Practice Vulnerability for Stronger Relationships* by Dr. Andra Brosh at www.healthway.com)

Now that you see the title of this chapter and the definition, what's going through your mind? Have I completely lost your attention?

I mean, who in the world would encourage someone to be vulnerable?
Especially women! Vulnerability has been viewed as being weak. We've been taught to keep it together in any situation without showing one ounce of fear. We've always had to keep it together emotionally.

Throughout my life, I've heard people say things like:

"Stop being so sensitive."
"Stop being so scary."
"That's too mushy."
"Be strong."
"Don't show your feelings."

Honestly, behind closed doors I desired to be all the things people were saying not to be.

Have you experienced times when you wanted to completely expose your flaws or fears, but just couldn't? Have you ever felt disconnected from those closest to you because you couldn't allow yourself to be vulnerable?

Well, I've experienced moments of being afraid of others viewing me as a weak individual. But then there's the side of me that was willing to take chances to make connections.

Let's begin by talking about what vulnerability looks like for me as woman. Naturally, I'm an introvert. I hate small talk. I enjoy lots of time alone! Although I enjoy socializing, it has to be meaningful. Any time I've had a great deal of social interaction, I have to go back into my shell to recharge.

Although I'm an introvert, I'm willing to take chances to initiate a connection. I feel as though we all have a desire to feel connected, but so many are too afraid to initiate a connection. I believe that if you never initiate a connection, you may miss out on opportunities to make amazing connections.

Secondly, I have a willingness to share my flaws openly. There seems to be so many barriers that keep people from sincere connection, barriers such as race, religion, financial status, politics, mommy competition, and perfectionism. My desire is to share my imperfections so we can all see each other as beautiful human beings.

Lastly, I possess a willingness to go above and beyond to keep a connection. I believe everyone desires to know someone is thinking of them, so I'm intentional about remembering birthdays, anniversaries, and special occasions.

Marriage

Shawn and I got married on a beautiful day in July. Well, let's just be honest, it was actually a hot and rainy day in July. Any day in July in Florida is H-O-T! But because I was marrying the most amazing man in the world, the day was beautiful. It was just a hot, beautiful day. HA!

I want to share a glimpse of what vulnerability looks like in my marriage. In my marriage, vulnerability is being willing to initiate the hard conversations. You see, it's the areas that automatically make me feel afraid, insecure, and angry. I'll touch on some of those areas as we go further into the chapter.

Secondly, it's the willingness to be honest even though there's no guarantee it will be reciprocated.

Also, it's learning to go through the process of having those hard conversations. It is developing the ability to be great listener, by learning how to listen without responding quickly. Aiming to understand what's being said and not just looking to respond. For Shawn and I, this has been an ongoing process. It's so easy to carry the weight of your feelings and respond out of those feelings without actually listening to what's been said. So, although I've found myself burning inside with a need to quickly respond, I've had to learn how to remain calm and quiet and listen. Whew! This has taken such a great deal of practice!

Lastly, vulnerability is a willingness to allow the hard conversations to be ongoing. It is so easy to assume that once the topic has been discussed, that's the end and it doesn't need to be discussed again. I've discovered that some conversations come in layers and require multiple conversations.

One of those hard conversations we had to have is in the area of our finances. Let me give you a little background. My husband is a spender by nature. He loves to spend money and large amounts at a time! I am the complete opposite. I dislike spending money. Well, at least in large amounts. I mean, I just prefer to spend in small amounts at a time.

I hate spending money on food, clothes, or shoes. The only time I enjoy spending is when I am giving it in some way. Strange, right?

With us being so different in the area of finances, you can imagine the tension it created from the beginning.

After constantly having disagreements over what we should spend and what we should save, I realized I needed to examine myself and try to understand the root of my issues. Why was it so hard for me to spend money? Why did I become so anxious when it was time to make a purchase? Why was I so irritable after a purchase was made?

The root of the issue was clearly fear. I dealt with this fear by being frugal. I became obsessed about his spending, because remember, he was a spender. I didn't trust his spending, which created a great deal of confusion, frustration, anxiety, and tension in our marriage.

A Wife's Superpower

What was I so afraid of? I was fearful that he was going to spend so much money that we would end up in a financial hole that we would never be able to get out of.

But, there was a bigger fear! I was afraid we would become homeless.

At some point, I had to make a decision to expose my fear to him. After initiating the conversation about my fear, this helped us communicate better about our finances. We had more freedom to discuss our finances and be productive in the discussion. It helped me to be more aware of that fear and what triggered it. It allowed for us to have an openness about my fear. Shawn could recognize when I was responding out of that fear. It allowed us to have a way to bring humor into a stressful area like finances. We learned to laugh. Lastly, it taught me to have realistic expectations about our saving and spending.

During my childhood, I didn't have the example of having those hard conversations. Once again, when I think of hard conversations, I think of those conversations that make you feel completely exposed. I wasn't shown how to talk about the areas that made me feel ashamed, insecure, or fearful. From one parent, the example I was shown was to suppress these types of feelings. From the other parent, the example I was shown was to verbally attack out of the feelings of shame, fear, and insecurity.

Although I didn't have the examples needed to gain the courage to have these types of conversations, I really desired to have the tools necessary to have a healthy marriage. I believe one of those tools is effective communication. As you can see, I didn't have a clue on how to go about getting these tools. I became determined to absorb more information about marriage, so I began reading articles as well as absorbing information from married couples I knew. I believe determination is what led me to gain the ability to be vulnerable in this way.

Postpartum

The hardest part of being a new mother is the feeling of being completely exposed to a world you know nothing about. This tiny little human is depending on you to know everything, yet you feel as though you don't know anything. You have to go through an enormous amount of trial

and error with almost everything. All while all
these questions swirl around in your mind:

"Is she eating enough?"
"Am I using the right brand of diapers?"
"Is she getting all the nutrition needed?"
"Have I taken every precaution necessary to
protect her from any harm?"

I ended up not being able to breastfeed, so I also
had to grieve the loss of breastfeeding. This loss
made me feel like a complete failure as a mother.
As you can imagine, this tormented me. There
were constant moments where I was feeding my
little girl with a bottle of formula, with tears
streaming down my face because of all the shame
I carried.

Let's not even begin to talk about the exhaustion.
It was more than I could ever put into words. My
hormones were going in every direction, it
seemed. I would lock myself in my bedroom and
cry into the pillow. Many times, I would speak
negatively about myself and my ability to be a
mother.

I was carrying all these feelings of shame, guilt,
and inadequacy, but instead of simply opening up

and being honest, I reacted by lashing out at Shawn. It could be the smallest thing that happened, and I would snap at him.

I was responding this way because I afraid to ask for what I needed. Here's what I needed:

*Time to be away for a least a few hours
*Regular time to shower without interruptions

*Time to eat without interruptions

*Time to simply do something I enjoy (ex: hobbies, read a book, listen to music)

*Time to invest in myself

I rarely asked for just a few hours away because I was afraid. Some people may be thinking, why would someone be afraid to ask that of their husband?

For me, it was fear that I was battling within myself. For example, I didn't want him to know how overwhelmed I felt most days because I was afraid he would think I was inadequate. There's such a tremendous amount of pressure on a mother to handle it all and handle it with perfection. I didn't want him to see that I was completely imperfect!

Inspired vulnerability in my marriage

I believe that my ability to be vulnerable inspired Shawn to be vulnerable, which inspired him to have the courage to make big changes. It was when I decided to open up to him and request his support. I was afraid to ask for his support, but I did. After trying to conceive a child for quite a few years and being unsuccessful, as well as seeing several doctors, those doctors explained to me that I could not conceive naturally. I decided I wasn't going to give up and would try something on my own, by drastically changing my diet. Taking that first step was a little hard and intimidating, so I asked Shawn to take the first step with me, purely for the support. He agreed, but only for the three days I requested.

At some point, Shawn began having some health issues that were linked directly to his weight. He carried lots of shame concerning his weight, so it wasn't topic that was open for discussion. Shawn saw such determination in me to get through the infertility, even through my feelings of hurt, disappointment, and shame. This inspired him to

45

face his shame, which was his weight. Shawn began opening up about how he felt about his weight and made a decision to go on the journey with me to completely change his diet.

Here are three practical ways to use Vulnerability to naturally and consistently draw the love you need from your husband:

1. Allow your spouse the liberty to be vulnerable by creating a safe space.

Show them that what they have to share matters by setting aside time to listen.

Be present in the moment.

Communicate back what they share.

Sometimes vulnerability doesn't mean or require talking. It could mean allowing the person to show emotion by tearing up or crying. It could mean just sitting in silence while they process their emotions. Sometimes just being there could mean and say so much.

There are times when your spouse needs a moment to be vulnerable, but you don't have time because you're working, in a meeting, or juggling the kids. An example of creating a safe place would be a quick call or text message, saying, "I love you." Or, "I'm so sorry I'm tied up at the moment, but I promise we will talk when I get a few minutes." Or, "Let's set aside some time this evening to talk." This allows that spouse to feel acknowledged as well as feel they have a safe space to be vulnerable.

2. Don't be afraid to ask for what you need.

Figure out what your needs are and initiate conversations about things you enjoy and your needs.

Believe that you deserve to receive what you need.

As women and/or mothers, we are known for being able to multi-task. We can be the driver, the chef, the cleaning service, the educator, the organizer, family facilitator, the scheduler, nurturer, financial planner, provider, and the caretaker; as we know, this list goes on for miles! But, we fail to let those close to us know we have needs that must be met as well. I had to stop believing that having needs meant being weak. I had to begin to believe that having needs only means walking out our humanity.

Sometimes, we just need time to be ourselves and do things we enjoy doing. You must believe that you deserve what you need. You are well worth it.

3. Believe in your spouse.

Let me start off by saying, I don't believe you can give what you don't have for yourself. In order for you to believe in your spouse, you need to be able to believe in yourself. This concept took me some time to grasp. I always cheered him on, but there was always a small percentage of doubt. It wasn't because he wasn't capable of doing whatever it was. It was because I carried doubts about my ability to do things. Also, I carried this fear of things just falling apart right before something good happened or before an accomplishment was reached. I had to tell myself, "Just believe, don't worry about the outcome." I observed that the more I believed in him, the more confident he became as my husband. Him knowing I was right behind him, cheering him on, kept him encouraged to persevere through some difficult times.

Melisha Singh

Personal Notes About Vulnerability

_____

_____

_____

_____

_____

_____

_____

_____

_____

_____

_____

_____

_____

_____

_____

_____

_____

_____

_____

_____

_____

_____

_____

_____

A Wife's Superpower

About Melisha Singh

My name is Melisha. I've been married to the most amazing man for 13 years. I have two beautiful children, whom I call my two miracles, ages five years and two years old. Several years prior to becoming married, I received a Bachelor of Science Degree from the University of N. Florida. I've been a stay at home mom for the last six years.

After years of being a stay at home mom, I've finally discovered that I aspire to uplift, inspire, and support the community of moms and wives by sharing my life through writing. I'm so excited about these opportunities to do so. Lastly, I'm a homeschool mom. This is a new journey for our family, but we are beyond excited about it. Who knows, we might just love it! I can be found on social media and via email at the following addresses:

Facebook –
https://www.facebook.com/melisha.r.singh
Instagram –
https://www.instagram.com/alittleloveatatime
Email – melisha.r.singh@gmail.com

Acknowledgements

First, I would like to thank my heavenly Father for giving me the ability to push beyond my fears and pursue this opportunity to share my heart. It has been an incredible journey.

I would like to thank my most incredible, brilliant, supportive, and loving husband. I love you, sweetie, and I truly believe you are my angel.

To my mom, who always found encouraging words that challenged me to be a good wife. I love you so dearly and feel so incredibly thankful for your words of wisdom.

A Wife's Superpower

To my family and friends, thank you so much for the many ways you've inspired me. I love you!

To Faith, thank you so much for believing in me. It will never be forgotten!

Chapter 4:
Emotional Intelligence

Teri Stewart

In our marriage, I possess a greater strength that is used for the betterment of our union. This is my Superpower, and her name is Emotional Intelligence.

What is Emotional Intelligence?[6] Emotional Intelligence is the ability to recognize and understand emotions in yourself and others. It's also your ability to use this awareness to manage your behavior and relationships.

I'm in an office meeting with my boss and a controversial question comes to mind; at my right sits Debating Dana and at my left, Complaining Carl. Emotional Intelligence tells me to hold my question until after the meeting and then ask my boss one on one, in order to prevent chaos from stirring in this productive setting.

Emotional Intelligence helps me understand how to fellowship amongst friends with different personalities. A topic is being discussed in a group setting and sweet Sara's body language shows she is uncomfortable with this topic, but she's not saying anything. Without being obvious, I instantly chime in and redirect the topic to create a more comfortable atmosphere.

I find myself in a familiar place asking the same questions:

Why do I have to be the strong one most often?
What about MY feelings?
When will he take one for the team?
Why do I have to be the bridge to amends?
It's not fair.
Am I apologizing first again, even when I'm not wrong?

Can you relate? Have you been there? It doesn't always feel good, does it? The famous question is WHY do I have to be this person? In the same thought, something in me knows these actions are necessary to hit the root of indifference and keep communication flowing in my marriage. Even when things do not unfold my way.

Paul and I have been married for nine years, with each year having its own set of peaks and valleys. I love being married to this man, having our family and all that comes with our Team. This life was not handed to us all put together; it's far from perfect. Please understand, a lot of work was and still is being put in, to create the life we desire, brick by brick. The sum total of our life is not our challenges alone; however, the process of overcoming these challenges reveals exactly what we are made of individually and collectively.

Two walking but only One agrees

Photography was an unspoken passion I quickly took notice of in Paul. On our first wedding anniversary, I surprised him with a Nikon camera. Without skipping a beat, Paul was all in. Classes, networking, educating, and learning... In a matter of months, we established a part-time photography business, which was unplanned and literally unfolded in a very short period of time. This was meant to be. It was an exciting season for us both.

Several years later, Paul expressed a desire to pursue our part-time business on a full-time basis. This meant leaving corporate America. We had several conversations surrounding this transition, but I was not feeling it. I was comfortable with consistency in income, paying all our bills on time, planning our vacations/holidays, and putting something aside for the unexpected. Not to mention, we enjoyed the extra income from the part-time business. Why mess this up? My eyes couldn't see the opportunity in going full-time. I only saw security being removed and that's about it. Paul was excited, eager to transition from corporate America. I, on the other hand, was not so eager. I became less vocal while determining how to process this expressed desire.

Rollercoaster

It is difficult to be in a place of agreement when your spouse is zealous and excited about the very thing you disagree on. Paul was at an all-time high in life. He uncovered a genuine passion with photography and the thought of pursuing this passion full-time would be his dream come true. At the same time, his desire to climb the corporate ladder was no longer, to the point he was downright miserable at the office. He yearned for my support in his passion and he received it with one exception—he couldn't quit his job in corporate America. We had a good thing going, but this began to cause a repeated rift between us. There was daily conversation with different approaches from him to convince me a full-time business would be a win, and a consistent "not right now" from me. He possessed a great deal of excitement about the possibility of full-time business, coupled with sadness that his wife was not on board. Excitement=Full-Time Business. Miserable=Corporate America. Brick Wall=Me.

Bridge over troubled water

I had many conversations with myself trying to understand my unwillingness to even consider the idea of him pursuing the business full time. Am I right? Am I wrong? Are my feelings about his passionate pursuit being weighed in? Coming into our marriage as a single parent, security was a huge priority for me and I was afraid the pursuit of a full-time business would somehow put us in a place of lack. It didn't matter how much we've saved, planned, etc. This was one equation I could not calculate, and it didn't make sense. I quickly identified fear as a leading factor in my non-budging stance and I did not want to admit this. Admitting this would communicate my perception of weakness, and my lack of trust and support in his vision. It just didn't make sense to me. I was not open nor was I in agreement to the transition toward full-time business.

A Wife's Superpower

Conversations began to transform into arguments, and expressions of my lack of support. Home became taxing in this season and it was not the happy place to be. We were becoming more and more distant, and our communication was being affected. Over a period of time, this got old and by being mad, arguing and not talking, walls began to form in our marriage. We were present, but it was cold, lonely, and very tense.

This was not a place I was willing to sit for long periods of time and I felt very passionate about it. Would we have disagreements? Absolutely—that is normal and healthy. Disagreements and not talking over periods of time was the more dangerous place for me to be. This was when I was talking to myself, my mad self, and thinking the worst. Recovery time needed to be quicker. Why were we arguing again? At some point, enough was enough. We could be mad at each other and in a place of disagreement, but together we would figure this thing out instead of living in division and not communicating. Stepping outside of my attitude for a minute didn't negate my feelings about the situation or remove the "I don't like him" at the moment. It simply meant I loved us more and that made it necessary that I take the higher road, extend the drawbridge, and work on us sitting on the same side of the argument.

Decide and Walk It Out

Our full-time business pursuit was one of the toughest seasons to work through in our marriage. We had discussed it so often, I became quiet and began listening more than voicing my opinion. The less I talked, the more it communicated to Paul that I was coming around. In reality, my stance had not changed.

I will never forget the day when Paul told me about a conversation he had with his boss about his season of working at the office being over. Paul shared that it was time for him to pursue his dream. He packed his items in a box and told his boss he needed to discuss with his wife before officially resigning. At that very moment, every emotion possible was taking place in my mind—anger, hurt, frustration, disbelief, and disappointment. He began to probe for my response. The only words I could muster were, "Give me 24 hours. I will respond then." There was nothing more I could say.

A Wife's Superpower

I needed a day to get my entire mind together. I was a mess and I was furious! How could my husband do this to me? To US? This decision would change our whole life and he told his boss before me?! REALLY!! Who cares that we've talked about it a number of times? At the point of decision, I should have been the first to know before any discussion took place at work. It was clear the decision had been made. It was also clear that I did not like how this was handled and tough conversations were coming. I had a LONG emotional night. Tears, toiling, and anger were taking turns with me. Journaling was my raw and uncut outlet; it allowed me to GET IT OUT the way I wanted to and needed at the moment, with a whole lot of uncensored emotion.

My feelings had to be shared on how this was handled before we could even discuss the decision. I felt blindsided. My trust was impacted, and this could not happen again. It was hurtful and disappointing. Along with walking out these changes, repair to this breach had to take place.

The decision had been made, so now what? For a moment, I entertained the idea. What if photography as a full-time business works? What if this is the best decision for our lives? Worst case scenario, he enters back into the workforce. Not the end of the world, Teri. I gave myself two options and silenced my fear, worry, and doubt. The options were: Fight it out with my "no" or give this opportunity a chance to work. This made it easier. Those 24 hours to get my head together were everything I needed to walk myself through a mound of emotions and find a piece of peace.

The follow up conversation took place the very next day. I made my feelings known about how this was handled. Apologies were extended and a commitment that something like this would not happen in this way again. Several conversations took place as a lot had to be unpacked from this situation. This transition was tough for me and every day was not excitement. The decision had been made and I would give this opportunity a chance to work. It still wasn't easy, but at this stage I agreed to walk this out. Eighteen months later, Paul Stewart Photography and our marriage are both thriving.

A Wife's Superpower

Observation

There are so many things I learned about myself in this trying season. However, it took more than love and more than prayer to navigate through this difficult situation. I often assessed my outlook and perspective before responding, even if that meant hitting a 24 hour pause to get my mind right. I questioned if I was being a brick wall and where my unwillingness to support this idea was coming from.

My heart wants him to be happy and to walk out his dream, and if, "No, not now," was my only response, then at a minimum, a plan of action needed to be considered. I want my marriage whole more than I want to have my way. I took on the role of bridging the gap and will continue to do so.

Emotional Intelligence as a Superpower is about apologizing first and acknowledging his feelings. I do what is necessary to create balance because my desires, voice, and opinions play a significant role if our marriage is to thrive. This will not always be an easy task but gets easier with practice.

Here are three practical ways to use Emotional Intelligence to naturally and consistently draw the love you need from your husband

1. Be aware of emotions, needs, and desires.
Knowing where I am and picking up on my spouse's emotions, needs, and desires is one of our strengths that keeps our communication growing. Sensitive topics should be addressed carefully. Understanding one another's triggers and how to operate when the triggers have been activated is key. "Not now" doesn't mean "no." If it's an expressed desire or need of my spouse, it's important, and it's equally important that I am instrumental in aiding with a plan for the expressed desire or need.

2. Pause before responding. At times of heightened emotions, this has been a lifesaver for both my spouse and me. Taking a few moments to settle those emotions and gain our bearings is sometimes all we need to move forward. This pause allows us to get to a place of talking and listening (communicating) instead of arguing our points. It's a cool down and should be used when necessary.

3. Move toward a quick recovery time. Address the issues at hand and forgive FAST. Too much time sitting in disagreement builds walls of division that are damaging to our union. The more we operate from a place of wholeness, the more we thrive in our marriage. It's okay to apologize first, be genuine, and move forward.

Teri Stewart

Personal Notes About Emotional Intelligence

About Teri Stewart

Teri Stewart is a native of Jacksonville, Florida. Married for nine years to her husband Paul, she is a mother of two boys, 20 and 16, and a bonus daughter, age 12. Teri is employed by AT&T full time and is Co-Owner of Paul Stewart Photography.

Teri is passionate about journaling, writing, and infusing others with positivity. Staying connected to strong women and women's empowerment has aided her in uncovering these passions. Her love for words inspires her to write and help others from her own experiences. IamSimplyteri.com is a blog she was inspired to create as a platform for herself while impacting others. Teri is a lover of people, welcomes new connections, and purposes to be a resource for others. Her smile best compliments her personality—happy, infectious, and infuses light in any room.

Stay connected with Teri via email info@iamsimplyteri.com or social media (https://www.facebook.com/Iamsimplyteri).

Acknowledgements

I would like to give honor to God for instilling in me the desire and determination to execute this project. Without HIM none of this would have been possible.

My loving husband, your support, encouragement, and believing in me has meant the world. I love you!

My friends and family, your support and cheering me on has been amazing.

To my fellow co-authors: We did it, ladies!!!

Last and certainly not least, my friend, my counselor, my superhuman, Faith. Words cannot describe my appreciation for you. Thank you for believing in me, catching my tears, holding my hand, and pushing me back in the ring.

A Wife's Superpower

This journey has been amazing, and I couldn't have done it without ALL of you. I love you...

Chapter 5:
Intuition

Natasha Redrick

It's early December and snowing. I'm in Alabama and, drum roll please, it's my wedding day!

I was marrying the love of my life. We had a fairytale courtship as high school sweethearts and maintained our relationship throughout our college years. It has now been fourteen and a half years since we said, "I do," on that cold and snowy December day. I can honestly say we still love each other deeply even though things have changed. We have grown, developed, and matured over the past fourteen and a half years. Has everyday been all wedded bliss, lovey dovey, this is the best day of my life? Absolutely not, but it has been an adventure of a lifetime that I would not want to do with anyone other than my husband.

Now, let's get to the reason I'm sharing my story with you. I have found my Superpower of Intuition to be more valuable than the most precious gem, and you can benefit from this inherent Superpower too. Here is my working definition of intuition so you are clear about what I mean when I use the word: Intuition is defined in the dictionary as one's ability to understand or sense something immediately without need for conscious reasoning.

Understanding or sensing something immediately—that is me. I pride myself on being very in-tune with the emotions, energy, and vibes of people. Since childhood I remember having a heart for people and the ability to feel other people's emotions. I would cry when they cried, whether I knew them or not. I genuinely celebrate people, including those I don't even know, for their accomplishments. Easily connecting with people, being relatable, and being intuitive are characteristics that mesh very well together. They go hand in hand and speak clearly to the person I am today.

At a young age, I noticed that I sensed things about people quickly without discussion or reasoning, but of course, I did not call it "intuition." It was just me being me I thought, but you will see that this is potentially you as well. I could talk with someone for a few minutes and understand them. Not by what they said, but by way of the "vibe" or "energy" they exhibited, which is more transparent than words, body language, and facial expressions combined. Initially, this feeling or intuition was a bit scary and I almost dreaded meeting new people, because I knew I'd be able to pick up on their "vibe" or "energy" very quickly and with minimum conversation on my part. As I got older and matured I realized my intuition allowed me to determine whether I wanted to spend my time around and establish a friendship with someone based on my intuition. I also came to understand that this Superpower warns me of unsafe situations and persons with ill intentions, so I began to appreciate its protective powers as well.

Because I have a heart for people, it has been and still is a challenge for me to not be a "fix it" person! Over time I started to understand it was not my role to take ownership of the problem, but to acknowledge it by way of validation and then direct them to the One I know is able to help and guide them, and that is God. This has been a lesson I use in my marriage as well.

With my husband, I always knew he had a good heart and was genuinely a kind person. He would go out of his way to help others or was always willing to lend a helping hand where needed. My intuition regarding him was always good back then and better now after learning more about him. Even when we disagreed often, I knew he was coming from a good place.

In the beginning we did disagree often. I had my way of how things should go, and he had his way. Because we were young and immature, we both wanted our own way and found it hard to joyfully compromise. Things like holidays, children, education, finances, renting or buying, cash or credit became points of contention in our relationship, but I never doubted or felt that his heart was anything but pure.

Once when we were car shopping, my husband, with his good heart and finance background, found the perfect car brand for our family in his head—yep, in his head (stop laughing). Now, I'm not an over-the-top-wife, have to have all things luxury or top of the line this or that, but I am practical. I also know and believe the old adage, "You get what you pay for," is true. So, he pleaded his case on this brand of cars based on how they are affordable and offer a one hundred thousand mile warranty, acknowledging that he knew we wouldn't keep this car long—maybe two, three years tops. On the inside I was all hot, mad, and bothered because guess what, I didn't want the car he was trying to convince me we needed to get. I was feeling like I work and contribute financially to our household just as much as he does, and this was not the car I wanted!

I was pouting like a baby because just for a moment, I wanted him to know that I was not happy with the direction this car situation was going. Now, you and I both know that pouting as an adult is not how you get things done; however, early on in our marriage that is what I did. In that moment, I didn't care about adulting. I cared about getting my way!

After I calmed myself down and sat quietly with rational thoughts going through my head, I said something to the tune of, "Babe, I think we are settling and we're paying for something you and I ultimately don't want." I shared with him that I heard and understood everything he'd said about the affordability, warranty, and not keeping the car past three years. However, I felt like we were settling and in the long run would both regret the decision. Resentment, or animosity, could slowly creep in and start to brew.

A Wife's Superpower

I then started to communicate as an adult and spoke to the heart of who my husband is. My intuition was screaming: All he wants is to protect and provide for you and his family. That's when and how I spoke to his heart. I acknowledged how he was a great provider for our family and how I appreciated him going to work every day (although in our household him working was an expectation unless we decided otherwise). It is still important to recognize and verbalize your appreciation to your husband, just as you want appreciation for your contributions. I acknowledged and shared how I appreciated him knowing that our old car was no longer dependable and how he had researched and devised a plan of action to get us a dependable and affordable vehicle. The more I spoke to the heart of who he was, the more I could feel his heart begin to open up, his eyebrows soften, and his charming smile slowly come through.

I was getting through to him. YES! I shared how I know another popular brand of cars had a long track record for dependability and affordability, and how I thought we would both like the vehicle. My husband was now all ears. I asked if he would be open to looking at this brand of cars and seeing if it was something he thought we could financially handle, and he gave an emphatic YES! In that moment my husband looked at me, held my hand, and thanked me for being his partner. He apologized for making me feel like I didn't have a say in the car situation. He ended by saying what my intuition had already told me, which was, "I only want to make sure we have a safe car for you and the children, so I don't have to worry about you all being stranded anywhere when I can't get to you." What my heart heard was protector and provider, and that was the beginning of me allowing my Superpower of Intuition to support my husband and raise our children as well.

When it comes to using intuition with your husband, you have to really know and observe him. Things like how he looks when he's in deep thought or how his breathing pattern changes when he's excited, all play a part in allowing your Intuition Superpower to lead in your relationship.

The conversations I initiated with my husband that did not go well were almost, bar none, when I wasn't leading with my Intuition. I had been so interested in having the conversation, getting my points of view across, and being heard that I'd missed the stoic look, the rigid posture, and the lack of eye contact during my plea for what I wanted. How have those conversations gone? you ask. Let's just say we had what my husband and I have termed "intense fellowships" with each other. Those "intense fellowships" often led to blame, resentment, unkind words, unmet goals in the marriage, and the list goes on and on. My intuition has taught me to observe nonverbal cues such as posture, facial expressions, tone of voice, body language, and energy vibes when he's talking about something happy, exciting, and joyous before jumping into a serious or difficult conversation. When I do, it alleviates a lot of the "intense fellowships" (intense fellowship is another way of saying heated argument when emotions are flying high) that we've had in the past.

One of the greatest blessings about intuition comes because you can perceive the energy or vibe of a person and tell right away when the timing is most likely to be the best to have certain conversations and discussions. This ability leads to minimum frustration and more pleasant marital experiences.

An example of using my Superpower of Intuition with my family was when my husband and I were actively seeking a regular babysitter for our children. We had received recommendations from friends who had used various people for different babysitting needs. We scheduled interviews and prepared questions that my husband and I thought would give us insight into the true essence of these women. We interviewed one woman and my intuition said stoic, likes children but not nurturing, firm but not playful. It wasn't that she didn't answer all of the questions correctly; it was just something about her that I couldn't put my finger on, but it made me feel a bit uneasy. When she left our home after the interview, my husband asked me what I thought, and I was completely honest with him, primarily sharing with him that it was something about her energy or vibe that just didn't sit right with me. My husband stated, "It's funny you say that because I felt the exact same way." It was just something I couldn't put my finger on with her even though she answered all the questions, smiled, and provided references as we requested. We eventually met and interviewed the woman we still use today as the babysitter for our kids. My intuition said grandmotherly, kind but firm, energetic and loving. Our kids still enjoy when she comes over to watch them and often ask when she is coming back.

A Wife's Superpower

Here are three practical ways to use Intuition to naturally and consistently draw the love you need from your husband:

1. Listen with your HEART (what is your spouse not saying?), not with your ears.
Verbalize your appreciation and acknowledgement of what your spouse didn't say with uplifting and supporting words. Remember, when using Intuition, you can feel or get a sense of the energy your husband is exuding in a conversation or situation. It is important to speak to the heart of what your spouse is not saying. When connected with someone on a spiritual and emotional level, you intuitively know their patterns and the rhythms of what they do and say.

2. Observe your husband's tone of voice, facial expressions, body language, and energy vibes when he's talking about something happy, exciting, and joyous. You may have to actually write down his tone of voice (high, medium, or low); facial expression (smiling, raised brow, shaking his head); and body language (open hands, clinched fist, leaning forward, lying back). These careful notations will be key in identifying the best time to have a more serious or difficult conversation. If time is of the essence and you can't wait to have an important conversation, even though it doesn't seem to be the right time, I recommend what I shared in tip number one. Listen with your heart and not your ears, to what your spouse is not saying. Lead with massaging his heart and state your observations in a loving and affirmative tone.

3. Trust what your intuition is telling you. It will never misguide you. The uneasy feelings or the warm fuzzies you feel with certain people or in certain situations are clues that guide you. They are the yellow light in your life that signal for you to proceed with caution or the green light to proceed without inhibition. Whatever the clue, TRUST your intuition.

Ladies, my prayer is that this chapter has confirmed what you already know about Intuition and has given you the tools you need to lead, observe, and trust that which is already inside of you. As I'm sure you already know, marriage is hard work with tremendous payoff. Intuition is a great gift, and when used to lead in your marriage, its value will exceed anything money can buy. I encourage you to use and rehearse these tips as you make your marriage the best it can be, using your Superpower of Intuition.

Personal Notes About Intuition

_____

_____

_____

_____

_____

_____

_____

_____

_____

_____

_____

_____

_____

_____

_____

_____

_____

_____

_____

_____

_____

_____

_____

About Natasha Redrick

Natasha Redrick, The Fundamental Mom, teaches moms principles that will lead to a more fulfilled motherhood and family experience. On Wednesdays, Natasha hosts a weekly video segment where she provides fundamental tips to moms on topics, such as how to: make memories during the summer, get kids drinking more water, and date your husband after the kids.

As a wife of fourteen and a half years and a mom of two amazing children ages seven and ten, she has a passion for moms and uses her experiences and knowledge to serve and empower them to get the most out of motherhood. She has worked with moms and their children in the area of nutritional counseling and mentoring for over thirteen years and brings a wealth of parenting information along with her.

In 2018, The Fundamental Mom launched its one year coaching program. This coaching program teaches moms how to live and have a more meaningful motherhood experience with their families based on the fundamental principles of value, voice, and one's village. If you want more out of your motherhood experience and have a desire to get back to what's most important to you as a mom, The Fundamental Mom is here for you!

Natasha obtained a Bachelor's degree from Tuskegee University in General Dietetics, is a Certified Lactation Consultant and an active member of Friendship Community Church. In her spare time, she can be found reading, journaling, shopping, crafting, and making memories with her family.

You can reach Natasha by visiting her website at www.thefundamentalmom.com; on Facebook: The Fundamental Mom; Twitter: Fundamental Mom; and Instagram: Fundamental Mom.

Acknowledgements

First, I have to acknowledge the One and True Living God, for without Him I am nothing but with Him I can do all things! He is my Rock and my Source and for that I am thankful.

To my husband Jerron, wow! I couldn't have asked for or dreamed that our God could have given me a better supporter, lover, partner, but most importantly BEST FRIEND! You absolutely ROCK and I'm thankful to God for ordaining and sustaining our marriage. I love you now and forever!

To my mommy and daddy, thank you for your example of marriage. You blessed me with a great foundation and instilled in me that God has to always be a part of anything that I do.

To Belle and Daddy Ralph, thank you for cultivating the principles of manhood, honor, and respect into my hubby and your son Jerron.

Now, to my two sweet potatoes, Niles and Nilah, I'm so blessed to be your mommy! Thanks for your hugs, kisses, and encouraging words. Your hearts for God, your infectious laughs, and your genuineness are all traits that I pray you both have throughout your lifetime. Mommy loves you both so very much!

Faith, thank you for this opportunity to share my marriage journey. To think that our first conversation was in the parking garage and to look at our friendship now is nothing short of God's divine plan for us! You are AMAZING, and I'm so excited about this book and the lives it will bless.

Chapter 6:
Identity

Heather Ross

I am Heather Ross and I demonstrate a tough exterior but, really, I'm pretty soft and my feelings can be easily touched by those I love and respect. I'm pretty in tune with my emotions and allow myself time to process whatever feelings I may have. I am fiercely loyal to those who are in my circle. I am that girlfriend who will be like, "Where they at? Let's go handle that," even though I've never been in a physical fight in my life.

I love to laugh and have fun. Food is a heavenly experience for me; and please, don't make me have to skip my morning coffee! Although I will, because I refuse to allow anything like that to control me.

I can be serious, sometimes too serious, so I have to remind myself it really isn't that serious and to enjoy the moment, because once it's over, it's only a memory.

A Wife's Superpower

I'm feisty and can be quick with my tongue, so
I've learned to pause before responding. But
pausing isn't my default or natural response; it is
a learned behavior. It's like that wild horse you
tame but have to keep a close eye on; otherwise,
they'll revert back to their nature. Yeah, that's me
and my mouth.

I am objective, and if I'm not cautious, I can
come off as argumentative or negative. I tend to
see things from a different perspective, especially
if I don't have respect for your way of thinking.

I am these things and so much more, but at my
core, I'm an authentic, passionate fighter. I'll
fight for my family, for justice, and for what is
right. If you take this God-given characteristic,
mix it with bitterness and resentment, add the
man I married who spent the majority of his
childhood and adolescent years fighting to be
heard, then you get several years of hurt, feeling
unheard, and unloved.

My story isn't one of marrying prince charming
and riding off into the sunset to live happily ever
after. It is, however, one of enduring love,
wins/losses, hurt, pain, healing, tenacity, and the
return to my true self. It is one of true love that is

unconditional and gives even when it isn't reciprocated. It is one of strength, and power, and beauty. Yes! My story is beautiful because it's mine, and I hope you find the strength and beauty in your own story as you read.

Our first eight months of marriage were great, as the honeymoon should be. We purchased a home and were settling into life together. We were excited about this journey and ready to take on the world. We had plans and quickly started executing them. Then I got the call saying he'd been released from his job. (Yes, he actually broke this news to me over the phone! I can laugh about it now, but it wasn't funny then and from there it was a downward spiral of financial woes and tension.) As a result of this tension, I began to see the other side of the man I married, as well as a side of myself I didn't want to own. I married a man with a BIG vision. That was one of the things that attracted me to him. I didn't realize that vision wasn't balanced with the understanding and practical execution of time and patience. He wanted his life of entrepreneurship and freedom, and he wanted it yesterday.

This led to several decisions that put us in financial hardships. I could see we needed to change our approach to moving forward and stabilizing our finances, so we could be in a good position to pursue entrepreneurship. The first few times we had this conversation, it was calm, and nothing changed. So the conversations got more intense. My tone grew sharper. My respect for him was declining, and my defenses were going up. I felt like I wasn't being heard and that my perspective was unappreciated. I didn't understand how he couldn't see the damage he was creating by continuing down this unproductive and financially crippling path.

Then the babies came, and I quit my job to be home with them. Not the smartest move on my part at all! We ended up having to sell our house or face foreclosure (we did a short sale) and eventually ended up in a place going week to week and not knowing how we'd eat. Thank God for a supportive family! We had years of financial struggle and couldn't seem to get on the same page about how to climb out of the hole, and in the midst of all of this was my wounded heart.

My husband prioritized his vision, his new business venture, and his hustle over me. He would spend countless hours working with business partners, developing plans, and attending meetings, and he was so energized by it all. I was always amazed at how dedicated and committed he was to the pursuit of his purpose and wished I could get an inkling of that desire sprinkled my way. I was second, and I didn't like it and started to resent it and him. I can recall countless times of earnestly asking him to love me the way I need to be loved. I made a list of things that speak to me and asked him to set his phone to remind him to communicate his love to me in some way. I sent him articles, we read books together, and I gave him hints—and still, nothing. I asked him to think about his family and talk with me before making financial moves on a business venture. I didn't want to control things, but in the spirit of partnership, I wanted to have input on these decisions because, inevitably, I would feel the impact. I wanted him to let me in on every level and he just couldn't seem to do so. It was like he was okay with only allowing our intimacy to go so deep, but I knew there was more, and I wanted it.

We would talk; I would cry. He would do better for a week and then it was back to the same ole, same ole. Eventually, I stopped crying. I started building a wall around my heart and started contemplating more and more about leaving his ass! (Yes, that is what I felt. Ass, not behind.) I started thinking about all the times my mom had told me not to let a man take advantage of me. I was raised to be an independent woman, told on numerous occasions, "Don't be dependent on any man. You position yourself to take care of yourself." Although there is some truth in that mindset, I used it as a tool against my spouse when he wasn't "acting" right. If he wasn't going to give me what I needed, I was not going to give him what he needed. *Shoot!* I thought, *He keeps playing, and he may have all the time in the world to focus on his dreams because the kids and I would be gone*, and I made sure he understood that!

This went on for years and the damage was compounding. He fought how he knew how to fight when he felt verbally attacked or unheard. This involved personal verbal attacks, like questioning my faith to believe, my strength to endure during a troubled time, etc. My husband is extremely optimistic and positive. So, from his perspective, if I would just get on board, see the future I desired and not lose focus, put my head down and get the work done, we would get through this tough time and be okay. We would start to build our empire! When I would come with my objective insight, realistic plans, and at times, accusatory ways, he saw that as me not believing, having weak faith, not partnering with him, not hearing him, and not believing in him.

If anyone knows me, they know I am a Jesus lover and my faith is my foundation. For him to attack what was most dear to me and discount the battles I'd won using my faith, those were fighting words! I would argue my position, not working to get a resolution, but to prove my point. I was fighting on the outside, but on the inside his words were causing me to question myself. Internally, my fight wasn't kicking in. I began to question if I knew how to do this wife thing. Maybe I did need to be more positive and dream a little bigger? I couldn't grasp why, if he felt that way, he didn't want to help me be better and grow in this area. I fell into a really dark place. We were under very hard financial strain. I was home with these beautiful babies and going crazy (I am SO not cut out for the stay-at-home-mom thing). I didn't feel as if my husband saw me as his partner or his equal, and I didn't feel like I was his priority.

A Wife's Superpower

I wanted him to do like the Bible said and "wash me with the water of the word." I wanted him to affirm me and speak life over me, to encourage me to up my dream game. I wanted him to let me partner with him in building his empire and not take my objective perspective on things as me being unsupportive or not believing. I wanted him to let me in and open his heart to me at the deepest levels. I wanted him to do and be all this for me, but I didn't realize I wasn't doing and being all for him.

Then the hard work began on my part. I started reminding myself of how smart I was, that my perspective was to be celebrated and considered, and that I was worthy of love. Don't sleep on positive affirmation because it truly works. You truly are a sum total of the thoughts you think! I went back to work—yes, Jesus! Although it helped my family financially, I primarily did this for me. In my role as wife and mother, I'd lost a huge part of myself that likes personal time and having something that is completely for me. At times, I would feel guilty for not being more present with my children, but I also understood that I was a better me, wife, and mother when I had time away from them and the gratification of my own personal accomplishments outside of them.

I started setting healthy boundaries for myself and my husband, and stopped building the wall around my heart. A boundary can be moved and re-positioned, but the only way to get rid of a wall is to tear it down. Setting healthy boundaries allowed me to still protect my heart while giving my husband an opportunity to show me something different so the boundary lines could be moved. For example, I shared with him how I didn't see him as a safe place to be vulnerable and "naked" (completely raw and truthful), and until I saw change in how he handled me sharing my fears and challenges, I would no longer share them. I told him the person I would share my vulnerabilities with until things changed for us and made sure he agreed with my choice. Even in this, I wanted to honor him as my husband. This was an extremely important step in my healing process because I reset the standard of how I was going to be treated.

As I came back to myself, I realized that I had not given my husband a soft place to land. When he had hurt me, immediately I threw up the defenses and made sure he understood it. As much as I was pleading for him to give me his heart and partner with me, I had been unwilling to provide a safe environment for him to do so. I began to see that when my behavior or tone reflected his past experiences, he reverted back to what he knew and would be on the attack. His relating to me in this manner also didn't help him put his defenses down so he could share his heart. His hurt ran much deeper than mine, and although I felt he should be working to right this wrong with me, in this instance, I chose to be the one to extend grace and love.

As I continued to work on myself and stay true to my authentic characteristics, an amazing thing happened. My husband started to reciprocate the love I was extending! He respected my boundaries but didn't want to be on the outside of my feelings, so he changed the way he communicated with me and how he handled my vulnerabilities. It was baby steps but, unlike before, they were consistent. He was checking in on me and expressing his desire to get "us" time in. He expressed he wanted me on his team and wanted to build this vision together. I was more open to being who he needed me to be within the context of who I am. We've started honoring and respecting who we are individually and who we are as husband and wife. It's a continued work, however, we've grown so much, and I am so thankful.

As I continue on this journey, I will not deny who I am but will always work on being the best me God created me to be. In your journey, I want to encourage you with these three tips to draw love from your husband.

A Wife's Superpower

**Here are 3 practical ways to use Identity to
naturally and consistently draw the love you
need from your husband:**

1. Don't lose your identity. You have
remarkable and powerful traits. Embrace them!
This is obviously a lot easier said than done. I
realize that you may be battling fear, uncertainty,
pain, and emptiness. However, let me tell you
that those feelings are only experiences that have
come from your journey, but should not define
the YOU in this journey. Life is our gym for
development and your marriage is the personal
trainer designed to show you what you are
capable of. If you're unsure of who you are and
have no idea where to start, take a look in a
mirror and ask yourself, "Who do you think you
are?" Have a pencil and paper handy as I want
you to write down everything that comes to mind.
Don't hold back from any good or bad that comes
out. You need to flush out your thoughts of
yourself because you'll find that what you think
of yourself is the person you give to the world
and more importantly to your marriage.

Once you've done this part, ask the people you
trust and are close to you, what type of person do
they think you are? What would you say are
healthy attributes you've had since childhood?

Once you're confident in who you are, fight to stay true to it, regardless of what anyone says and the circumstances you face.

2. Set healthy boundaries. Let's be sure we understand what a healthy boundary is. A healthy boundary is you positioning your expectations about a particular matter based on an understanding and clear communication. We get off track in our marriages by having expectations about things that we never got an understanding of or full clarity about. Just because you grew up a certain way, it doesn't mean your spouse will see things similarly. There is nothing wrong with letting a person know your expectations for how you will be treated and what is allowable when in relationship with you. Be courageous and speak up! This allows you to protect your heart and feelings when dealing with unhealthy situations. It also sends a strong message to your partner that you have a standard and they have to meet it, or they will not be allowed in that area.

3. Check yourself. Don't allow your influential characteristics to go unchecked and be used to hurt others. When you step outside of the goodness of your identity, it's dark, ugly, and damaging. Know that you and you alone are responsible for your heart no matter what. At the end of your day, evaluate your responses to your spouse and what motivated them. Did you do things to encourage, to motivate, or to give a different perspective? Or was it done in spite, to hurt, or even defend? If your actions didn't come from a healthy place, why? What can you do differently? Do you need to set some boundaries? Do you need to speak to someone professionally? These are the conversations to have with yourself, and be honest with yourself about where you are.

My Superpower is my identity. I know who I am, and I know the power I possess. Who are you?

Personal Notes About Identity

_____

_____

_____

_____

_____

_____

_____

_____

_____

_____

_____

_____

_____

_____

_____

_____

_____

_____

_____

_____

_____

_____

_____

_____

_____

About Heather Ross

Heather Ross is a passionate and strong woman who enjoys living life to its fullest and relishing in the fact that she is lavishly loved by a Good Father. Born in Mississippi but raised in Georgia, she's enjoyed the closeness of her family and the security that comes from her tribe. As a result, she is passionate about marriage and family and works with other couples to help strengthen this beautiful institution through various fellowship groups. She believes couples should connect with other couples because no one and no relationship was created to be an island unto itself.

She's spent the past 13 years working in higher education as a program coordinator/manager and has the benefit of sharing life skills and job training with her student assistants. In her spare time, she loves traveling, eating, watching a good movie, and creating memories with her family.

She and her husband, Curtis, have been married almost 11 years and have two beautiful children, Hailey, age seven, and Camden, age four.

You can reach Heather at hmross07@gmail.com.

Acknowledgements

I couldn't start this without first giving thanks to my Father God for seeing me as He created me to be and loving me every step of the way. My identity truly is in Him alone, and as a result, I am who I am.

To my best friend whom I get the privilege of calling husband and lover (uhmhmm!), thank you for being my sunshine on a rainy day. I am grateful for your commitment to me and our children and for loving us the unique way you do. I love you, babe!

A Wife's Superpower

To my village (Mommy, Tisha, Antwone, and my fam/friends), life wouldn't be half as great if you weren't in it, so thank you for walking this thing out with me.

To my "safe person," Toya Hayes. Girl, I wouldn't even be a part of this great project if you weren't there to talk and pray me back to my senses. I love you so much!

Faith, you are an absolute rock star! Thank you for believing in me, guiding me, and encouraging me through this process. Because you saw what I didn't even see, great things were birthed in me. I bless you and love you.

To all my sisters who are a part of this project, job well done! As a result of your transparency and openness, changing the lives of so many people has begun.

Chapter 7:
Silliness

Keisa Campbell

September 11, 1999, was the day that one of my dreams would come true. It was 87 degrees on a beautiful sunny day. The trees were still green and not a gray cloud in the sky. The weather was perfect for the day that I became a wife. The thing is, I almost didn't walk down the aisle. Suddenly I wasn't sure—not nervous, just wasn't sure. I knew I really loved him and wanted to be with him, so I didn't know where the uncertainty was coming from. You see, I was only 21 years of age, very young, I might add, to be called someone's wife. I wanted to spend the rest of my life with this man, with no blueprint, manual, or example in my family on how and what it took to be a wife. I can remember my mom saying to me, just before she was escorted into the church, "Young lady, I hope you know what you are doing." I just smiled and then uncertainty set in even more.

I later realized that I married my best friend on that day. I didn't know at the time that he would become my best friend. I knew how he cared for me when I was a teenager having panic attacks while we both worked at Six Flags Over Georgia. I had to be taken to see the nurse because of my panic attacks, and he would be right there, showing me he cared about me early on. He was concerned about what I ate and wanted to be sure I wasn't eating crap, as he would call it. He made sure I got home from work, and when school started he would pick me up, often having food in the car, or we would stop to get something before he took me home and went to work.

As a woman, I am gifted with so many Superpowers. For years I thought encouragement was my Superpower because that was something I did naturally. My family appreciated me encouraging them in what they wanted to do, but that was not my Superpower. I later learned that silliness is my Superpower.

I can't recall the exact year I discovered silliness as my Superpower, but I sure do remember the effect my Superpower had on both my husband and my girls. My family is naturally silly, and I'm the one who keeps things in line. I'm the one who asks what are the plans for the future and what has been done to accomplish them. My family often questioned why I was so serious all the time. I didn't think I was, but apparently to my family I was.

One day I saw how my husband responded to me being silly, something that I didn't do very often. I was dancing and being goofy at the same time. He just watched me and laughed, and next thing I knew, he was all over me like a Cheshire cat. He started tickling me like I was a Pillsbury dough boy. Then he pinned me down with one hand and held me while continuing to tickle me and kissing me, and then what happened: hot sex! Now, if someone would have just told me right off the bat that dancing and being goofy would lead to passionate, hot sex a little earlier, I would have done that!

It not only led to passionate sex, but sometimes it also led to great conversation. I remember my husband opening up about some fears he had that I had no idea about, but we were able to talk about those things in depth. I appreciated those moments because it wasn't that often, at the time, that he would open up. It was like my silliness opened the door for him to be free to share some things that were on his heart.

What I noticed about using my Superpower is that it influenced my husband. As I mentioned earlier, my husband gets turned on when I act silly and often joins me and replicates my moves. I remember one time he was lying on the bed and I came in the room dancing goofy. He lay there watching me and laughing, and said, "This doesn't bother me. I love it when you are silly. I only wish you would do it more often." That was a lightbulb moment for me. What I realized in that moment was that I don't always have to be serious or have so much going on that I can't share the whimsical side of myself with the ones I love. I believe I had become so fixated on being the best this or the best that, that I forgot it was okay to just be present with my husband and allow myself to be vulnerable.

I know that laughter is contagious, and when I laugh I decompress. I use this Superpower as foreplay with my husband and as a way to spend more time with my family; it seems to bring us all together. Silliness has multiple benefits in my household. It not only leads to hot sex, but the laughter it promotes in my home is priceless and good for the soul.

Here are 3 practical ways you can use Humor to naturally and consistently draw the love you need from your husband:

1. Be spontaneous. If you feel the urge to do something silly, just do it.

2. Don't take yourself too seriously or worry about what others are going to think. It's okay to let your hair down and act like a fool. If you enjoy dancing like I do, then just get up, bust a move, and be real silly with it.

3. Unplug from social media. Create situations where your hubby can laugh until his belly hurts.

Personal Notes About Silliness

_____

_____

_____

_____

_____

_____

_____

_____

_____

_____

_____

_____

_____

_____

_____

_____

_____

_____

_____

_____

_____

_____

_____

About Keisa Campbell

Keisa realized at a very young age that she was called to help others. She had her very own teaching session when she was around 10 years of age when her older cousin asked her to teach her how to plait hair. She had her very first coaching session while in high school when she found a gym teacher in the locker room crying and she was not only able to encourage her during that time but left such a lasting impression on her heart, that the gym coach attended her wedding years later. She realized her calling was to encourage, build and lift up women, and aid them in living a beautiful life.

A Wife's Superpower

Her love for wanting to help others, especially women, took her on her own journey of "Beautiful Living." She firmly believes women are more than just daughters, wives, and mothers. Keisa knows women also have dreams and goals that require planning, focus, and nurturing, and that beautiful living is accessible to all. She is dedicated to helping women overcome life's challenges and obstacles, discover their purpose, achieve work-life balance through self-care, uncover who they really are underneath it all, and show up with brilliance.

Keisa is a Certified Professional Life Coach (known as The Beauty and Transformation Coach), speaker, licensed hair stylist, image consultant, mentor, wife, and mother. She, like you, wears many hats and understands all too well the struggle of trying to balance it all without losing herself in the process. That used to be her story until she got really serious about "Beautiful Living." She teaches women how to live a beautiful life by being a living example and through speaking, coaching, and workshops. You can reach Keisa at www.keisacampbell.com.

Acknowledgments

First, I have to give honor to God who is the head of my life and thank Him for trusting me with his special assignment to serve others. I want to thank Him for the gifts and talents he has blessed me with and for continuing to give me the courage to move forward.

I also want to thank my family (Terrance, Bre, Teryn, and Kennedy) for supporting my hopes and dreams and for being there for me when I've needed you most. I love each of you.

I would like to dedicate this chapter to my family for allowing me to be vulnerable around each of you. At times it was hard for me to let go of everyday life and just enjoy the moment and be silly, but I realized that during those silly times we came together and had the best time.

I also want to dedicate this chapter to all the women who will read this. My prayer is that you will find time to not wear your title, but to let your hair down for a moment and out of nowhere just be silly.

Chapter 8:
Resilience

Colleen Taylor

"The process of adapting well in the face of adversity, trauma, tragedy or something stressful. To have the ability to bounce back no matter the situation."[7]

"Why the hell are you telling me I am resilient? Do you even know what it means? Is it not something that everyone has to be at one point or the other? Am I not just existing and taking life blow by blow like everyone? Why would I think myself to be any different from any average Joe walking past me?"

These are the thoughts that passed through my head over and over whenever I thought of my situation and circumstances and heard those words leaving from someone's lips. If you have had this same thought process, STOP IT!

Yes! I did just tell you to STOP IT! I am telling you this because it is something I had to tell myself. Don't get it twisted; I am not a mean person. I am a realist who has to pause to see things the way they really are.

I am not trying to be rude. I am trying to get you to understand you are an exceptional person to go through every situation you have been though and still find a way put self to the side and focus on being there for others.

My story may be different from yours, but only to a certain extent. Just as this book was guaranteed to be filled with words, your life is guaranteed to contain trials and tribulations at some point. The lady sitting next to you (yes, turn and look at her and say hmmm); the guy at the other table across from you; or the person you just passed on the way to sitting down to read this book have all experienced trials and tribulations. Let my little snippet of a story be a reminder that you have the power to be a resilient individual regardless of how big or small your situation. I want you to know that even when life comes at you "like a wrecking ball," you too can choose to be a resilient individual. It's an option that everyone has, yet many of us so often tend to bypass.

I'll start my own story off with a quick definition of what resilience means to me. I know my definition is a little unusual, but I am going somewhere with this. Upon reading the actual definition of the word, I realized my own definition. My definition was simple: ***I got hit by several dump trucks in life, yet still managed to crawl out from under them and kept moving, even if sometimes all I could do was limp***. In life, I have encountered sickness, financial problems, the loss of loved ones, challenges in my marriage, and many other things, but I was able to get through those rough patches no matter how difficult they were. Being resilient has less to do with the current situation a person is in and more to do with their character and how they respond to the situation they are dealing with. Everyone at one point or another will encounter life's challenges. It's not so much "what" we go through but "how" we get through it that makes us resilient.

My thought process…

I thought surviving years of abuse at the hands of an evil man (whom I would learn later was not my biological grandfather) proved I could handle any tragedies that life would throw at me. I became a somewhat functional adult, or at least that is what I thought. I mean, I managed to keep my sanity (chuckle). I thought being able to graduate high school, enter the military, get married (did I mention I never thought I would get married?), and have children despite it all was resilient. I entered boot camp one week after surgery without them knowing. Wasn't that resilience? I was able to bounce back from each of those situations and carry on with life.

Fast forward almost two decades later, I felt so caught off guard. I lost sight in one eye. Weeks later, I would observe my father-in-law take his last breath. Shortly after, my mother suffered a severe stroke and collapsed in my arms. I am going to throw in a scene for you to give you a picture of where my mental thought process was at this point. I am sure most have seen that stereotypical movie where that one character just will not die regardless of how many times you hit or shoot them. This is where my mental capacity was during this time. However, we all have a breaking point, and mine was swiftly approaching. The moment my mother recovered well enough to be on her own, my husband experienced what would be his first of numerous ambulance runs due to his heart.

This was all too much. It was easy to feel like I could conquer the world when it was only affecting me, but when it came to my children and my husband, my resilience had to grow to a whole new level. All of this was a form of resilience, but I didn't know how to convince myself of that. It's common for many of us to very easily look at another individual and call them resilient, but often fall short of doing this for our own selves. There were many days I had to look at myself in the mirror and tell myself I was a resilient person. When my husband ended up in the hospital, my resilience had to kick in overtime. I had to pull myself together and remain focused on the task that lay before me. What did this mean? This meant I had to be strong enough for the both of us. I could not fall to pieces; I had to remind myself that I was strong enough to handle this.

Everyone has the potential to reach a point where they are emotional, physically and mentally spent. Not all actually reach that point, but it does happen for quite a few.

Eventually we will all, at some point or another, have a moment (some more than others) where even the strongest of strong will hit a low point.

My breaking point came when I heard the words "quivering heart and surgery" uttered from the doctor's mouth. As the words met my ears, my breath fell to the bottom of my stomach. My breath could not escape my lungs. I was trapped in that moment, unable to breathe, unable to speak, unable to blink, unable to think, or to understand what I was hearing. I felt the air in my body slowly leaving, my knees buckling slowly to the ground. "Mrs. Taylor! Did you hear what I said? We need you to come with us immediately." My mother-in-law came up behind me and touched me gently to let me know she was there and help me pull myself together. I knew my husband needed my strength at that moment; it was not time to break down. Having a meltdown at this moment wouldn't be beneficial. My husband needed me to be strong and maintain self control. This was the time I needed to assess what was actually happening before me and all the possible scenarios that could play out.

We grabbed our bags and almost ran the doctor over trying to catch up to him. Within moments, the doctor began breaking down my husband's diagnosis and all of the different options for treatment that he recommended. When the doctor stopped speaking, all that lingered in the air was him telling me that my husband needed emergency open heart surgery because his heart could not beat on its own. Due to the urgency of the matter, he was given a few hours to allow his family members to see him in case the surgery was unsuccessful. Walking slowly down that ever-so-long hallway, I knew I had to pull myself together. His mother was right beside me. There was no time to fall apart. I had to be brave because my husband was looking up at me to see what was going on based on the response on my face.

Resilience was there… but so was anger and fear.

The thought of losing my husband became so real that I became angry. I was angry at knowing that he might leave me. He told me that he was "determined to live and come back to his family," but I had doubts. He could not control what was going on, and this truth was the fearful part! My fear kicked in when the doctor told me that his heart stopped several times on the table and his four-hour surgery had now become eight. I had hours to think about how he was fighting for his life. I had to remind myself of our conversation and prayers. He was fighting for his life, and I was fighting my thoughts. Everything was happening all at once, but I had to believe in our faith. My resilience caused me to push past my natural capacity and lean on God. I had to come to a point where it was no longer about me. Thinking back on it, we all will eventually get to that point at some time or another. My love alone could not get me through this. I had to rely on those around me to be strong for me. I yearned to hold him once again and to feel his soft lips against mine. I yearned for the distinct texture of his voice and to speak with him again. Letting go of my fears and anger, all I could do was cry.

As a resilient human, I gave myself permission to cry, laugh, dance, run, or whatever I needed to be me.

I had to give myself permission to cry and know that it did not mean I was weak. When I saw my husband lying there before me—hooked up to a life support machine breathing for him—I had to take a moment and let the tears flow out of me. It was all too surreal, to know that the man I had known for over 20 years may not make it through the night. The very idea that my children may have to say goodbye to their father was so heartbreaking. It hurt to breathe. It hurt to think.

A Wife's Superpower

The depth of my pain was almost too much to bear, but I had to dig in deep and realize that though my heart, mind, and soul may have been shattered for that moment, that was it! Just a moment! I gave myself permission to cry. My tears were not for me, but for what lay before me. No matter how much I wanted to cry for myself, my tears were for my husband and our children. I knew at that moment that things had changed, and I needed to process that. This release gave me the time I needed to recharge. Oftentimes, when I had something heavy on me, I was able to cry in my husband's arms, but this time it had to be done alone.

Your facial expression and body language are key indicators for what you are thinking.

I kept in mind that my facial response was a marker for what I was thinking. My husband always told me that my face was a telltale sign that something was wrong. This was not the time for that. I had to stay positive in order for him to stay positive. I told him he was going to be okay and that we had decades of celebrating we would partake in. This was only one more obstacle we needed to overcome. I had to believe in what I was saying, so he could believe in it too.

Believing in my husband was vital because it gave me the mindset I needed in order to be strong. My strength allowed him to be strong during his weakest moments because he was able to draw it from me. I learned it is very attractive to a man to know that his woman is able to go through a storm or endure a storm and get through it.

To be clear, my husband recently shared with me that he considered it "sexy" to know that he could depend on me in the darkest hours of his life. When my husband told me this, I was blown away. I was doing my best to keep it together in the midst of this crisis and manage the children, our families, the finances, doctors, mounting medical bills, etc. My husband shared that this gave him the strength and much needed tenacity to fight, not only to stay alive but to rebuild his health to a state where he could remove the burden off of me. He was inspired to combat this great "blow" to our family. He knew the potential to fall into severe depression as a result of the recent devastation. My husband would continually remind me that he couldn't possibly allow himself to sit by and watch me fight this storm by myself. He was inspired to think positively, to commit to both assigned therapies, and to research new opportunities that he would be able to do. He would watch positive videos. He would only read positive articles and posts on social media. If it was inspirational, he was on it. He was determined to make me cry at how great life had become one day. As he stated it, my resilience refueled his mission to be our "rock in the household."

Our children went from wondering how we were going to make it if "Daddy" was down, to having a newfound faith in "Mommy" being capable of running the show. Our daughter began to develop a passion for cooking, cleaning, and running her own business, all while being a nurse! Yes, it may seem like a lot, but it just happens to be the impact of what she had witnessed in us firsthand. She now sees that a strong woman can take care of her family and run it like a business. She understands the importance of a woman in the household and the world. At that time, it was the furthest thing from my mind, but it was something I have often thought about since.

Resilience sometimes mean you have to rationalize with yourself.

How do you move forward? It can be very difficult to not place blame on oneself or others when faced with extreme illness and/or potential death knocking at the door. No matter my past or present, it was not time to tally up receipts and verify records of who did what, when, why, where, and how. It was time to take "self" out of the equation and focus on moving forward. Getting my husband back was my main concern and nothing else.

Everyone needs time.

Situations will happen that are out of your control. Allowing yourself and those around you time for processing what happens (no matter how big or small) is a good way to grow and move forward. When my husband was going through various treatments and therapy, we all needed time to heal. We all needed to adapt and learn through all the different changes taking place. It was difficult and frustrating for everyone in our family, as we all had to find a new sense of normalcy. This could only be done over time. We had to find the humor in things that frustrated us and allow ourselves to laugh. This helped in cutting the tension in our home, and laughing together at each other allowed us to grow together, not allowing anyone to feel like they were a burden.

The recovery process is an ongoing thing that continues up to this day. There are moments when my "tank" gets low. Being resilient does not mean I am Super Woman. Regardless of what I may feel, if you ask my family they will tell you it's definitely considered my "Superpower." I have days when I need to talk to others to get that emotional buildup needed in order to make it through the day. A lot of times we put unnecessary pressure on ourselves to be something that we read or watch, although it may not have necessarily been modeled before us. Resiliency is not one of them; whether you are single or married, with children or without, we all have resiliency on the inside of us. We just need something to activate it and the skill to utilize it. Marriage is a major avenue in which your resiliency can be drawn out and strengthened.

Here are 3 practical ways you can use Resilience to naturally and consistently draw the love you need from your husband:

1. Resilience does not mean you cannot release.
Give yourself permission to cry, laugh, dance, run, or whatever you need to do to be you. It allows your spouse to see that you are human. Please don't allow yourself to think it means you are weak. Crying in each other's arms causes you to form a closer connection.

2. Monitoring your facial expressions is always necessary. My husband always told me that my face was a telltale sign that something was wrong. It is hard to convince your spouse that you are okay when your face is saying something different. Body language is often considered louder than verbal communication. Ask your spouse to give you gentle reminders when your face is saying something other than "it is okay."

3. Understand that additional emotions will come along with resilience. When common emotions such as anger and fear arise, talk about them. Do not keep negative feelings bottled up inside. Communication is vital in any relationship. When we express what we are

126

feeling, it allows us to be vulnerable to each other.

Personal Notes About Resilience

_____

_____

_____

_____

_____

_____

_____

_____

_____

_____

_____

_____

_____

_____

_____

_____

_____

_____

_____

_____

_____

_____

_____

_____

_____

A Wife's Superpower

About Colleen Taylor

Colleen Taylor migrated from Jamaica West Indies to Brooklyn New York at a young age, where only three years later she would meet Horace, her loving husband of twenty plus years. In 2018, Colleen obtained her Bachelor's degree in Business Management and Supervision after taking a seventeen year hiatus to raise four beautiful children: Anthony (20), Machai (17), Horace III (14), and Celine (13). Colleen is currently walking out her passion in Business Management for several private offices in her local area.

Driven by her passion of strategic building and structure, Colleen continues to seek new ways to encourage and grow herself and everyone with whom she comes in contact. Her contribution to this anthology has awoken a new beast which cannot be quenched with just one entry.

Stay tuned for more to come!
Email contact: restoredin2008@gmail.com

Acknowledgments

Gratitude is my start and finish. I am grateful to God for giving me the opportunity to be part of this dynamic group of lovely ladies.

I dedicate this chapter to the love of my life and best friend, Horace. You have always loved me past the depth of gravity and back. For that I am forever thankful. You have always been my guardian angel watching out for me and being my rock.

My dedication continues with my wonderful four children with whom God has blessed us. It is both an honor and a privilege to know I am your mother. Continue to start and finish strong in all you do.

A Wife's Superpower

To all my many family members and friends who continue to guide me on my path… thank you. You make this journey both exciting and interesting.

I would be remiss if I did not thank a special couple, Joseph and Corris Isagba. You have walked a path not travelled by many, and for this you both are inspirational all by yourselves.

We are all inspirational to someone in one way or another, and for that I am grateful!

Chapter 9:
Support

Earitha Anderson

Dwight and I met on a Friday night during a church service. I had worked late that day and arrived shortly after the service began.

Rushing into the service, I spotted my cousin and noticed an empty seat next to her. I quickly made my way over to where she was to claim my seat. We greeted each other, and she introduced me to "Uncle D." Dwight and I briefly exchanged hellos and I immediately engaged in the worship service.

As I stood, eyes closed, quietly praying within and feeling grateful I had made it to service, I heard a voice in the distance boldly extolling praises with an energy and excitement unlike anything I had heard before.

At some point, the voice became too distracting and I could no longer focus. It was somewhat annoying, yet absolutely captivating. On the one hand, I wished the person would worship quietly

within, kind of like I was, yet I was impressed by his ability to worship so freely in public.
I secretly wished I could experience his same level of freedom. I wondered who the person was. I didn't recognize his voice. I was curious about the person behind the voice that was so enthralled in worship.

Eventually, the suspense became so overwhelming I couldn't take it anymore, so I gave into temptation and opened my eyes. To my surprise, the voice I heard belonged to Dwight. There he stood, hands lifted, head tilted back with tears streaming down his face, totally immersed in spiritual bliss.

It was the most powerful visual I'd ever seen. My heart immediately melted, and I forgot all about my troubles.

The truth is that I was in a rough season of my life. I was on the verge of divorce and had become a workaholic. I worked all the time, so I wouldn't have to think about my life and the pain I was in. Church for me had become my place of respite and spiritual revitalization.

Eritha Anderson

Dwight and I quickly became friends. Some
didn't get our connection at first. They compared
our age difference, our economic status, and our
social status. Little did they know, Dwight and I
had many things in common: we had our faith
and spirituality, our passion for helping others,
our pursuit of purpose, and (this may catch some
by surprise) even our former imprisonment.

Dwight was a convicted felon who had spent
thirteen actual years in prison. Conversely,
having endured horrific abuse, I had spent a
lifetime in an emotional prison. After being
released from prison, Dwight relocated from
Tampa to Jacksonville to start his life anew. I was
starting my life over after a fourteen-year
relationship devastatingly collapsed and ended in
divorce. With the help of therapy, our faith, and a
great support system, we have each been able to
successfully overcome our former imprisonment.

SUPPORT[8]

According to FreeDictionary.Com, to support
something means to bear the weight of, especially
from below; keep from falling, sinking or
slipping. In that same context, support may also

mean to bear or hold up an amount of weight (as in a bridge being able to support five tons).

Over the next several months, our friendship blossomed. Dwight and I shared a mutually beneficial and interdependent relationship. We provided support to each other in many ways. He challenged me to become more spiritually aware. I helped him to become more adapted to a world he barely recognized or could function in.

Dwight's transition back into society after a thirteen-year absence was quite arduous. He needed a lot of encouragement and support to accomplish the most basic life tasks the majority of people take for granted.

For instance, at the onset of his incarceration in 1992, the personal computer was not common to every household, yet in 2005 when he reentered society, computers had widely become the norm and people used them for everything from research to applying for jobs, doing homework, and even paying bills. Dwight, who had never used a typewriter before, now had to learn both how to type and operate a computer concurrently.

One evening I stopped by his sister's home (where Dwight lived) for a visit. Everyone gathered in the family room engaged in conversation. Dwight motioned for me to come back to the computer room to help him with something. I followed him and stood in the doorway as he sat down at the desk.

Seemingly embarrassed and avoiding eye contact, he asked if I would show him how to use the computer. I knew it was selfish, but frankly, I had only stopped by for a brief visit that evening. I didn't plan to, nor did I feel like staying long enough for an impromptu tutoring session. But out of courtesy, I said yes and proceeded to show him some computer basics.

Dwight was having trouble keeping up and remembering what I taught him. Perhaps I had taken for granted that although using the computer was second nature to me it might take him a while to catch on. I really didn't want to continue, and eventually he sensed my agitation, became overwhelmed, and sat staring at the computer screen.

Fighting back tears, he began, "I really appreciate you taking time to help me. I'm not trying to make this difficult for you. This is just foreign to me, so I may not get it as quickly as someone else. I am working hard to do everything I need to do to start my life over. There's a lot to learn. I've figured out quite a bit on my own, but there are some things I still need help with. I didn't expect everything to be easy, and right now I feel a bit lost, but if you could grant me a little patience, I know I'll get there. I just need a little help." I listened, feeling perplexed and thinking to myself, *Dude, it's really not that serious. I'm only teaching you the basics.*

He continued, "Before I went to prison you went to a company, you filled out an application, and if they liked you they hired you. Or, if you knew someone who could put in a good word for you, nine times out of ten you got the job. Now, in order to get a job everything starts at the computer. Without it, I can't even make it to the application or an interview. I don't know anything about computers, but I have to find a job. Do you mind showing me how to use this?"

I have to admit, I was taken aback by Dwight's vulnerability. Until then, the only things we shared were church, great conversation, and a few meals. However, I wondered what caused him to feel more comfortable to ask me, an outsider, for help rather than his own family. On the other hand, why wasn't his family able to recognize his needs and support him in the ways he obviously needed to help him move forward?

He went on, "I feel like I stepped out of a time machine and suddenly found myself in 2005. So much has changed. Little is the way I remember it. I have pressure from probation, pressure right here (meaning his sister's home), and pressure from society." Tears now streaming down his cheeks, he shared, "Everyone keeps telling me **what** I need to do, **why** I need to do it, and **when** (how fast). I'm willing to learn, but no one seems to understand that the help I really need is with understanding HOW!"

Dwight was so overcome by emotion he stopped talking. For several minutes there was an awkward silence followed suddenly by an eruption of tears for what seemed an eternity. His loud cries eventually tapered into silent sobs until they too finally stopped. I tried to empathize, but I just wanted him to gather his composure before one of his family members walked into the room. I was too afraid they might try to link us together or make us the brunt of their jokes.

138

A Wife's Superpower

For a while I was reluctant to offer any help to Dwight. Sometimes I purposely avoided him, so I wouldn't have to answer his questions, give him advice, or show him how to do something.

One day I recall getting a phone call from Dwight asking if I would be willing to open a bank account for him in my name. I was flabbergasted. I couldn't figure out why he wanted someone he'd known for a relatively short time to handle his personal business matters. Apparently in Dwight's past life, he had never opened a bank account before. He would have women he knew or dated open a bank account in their name and handle all of the transactions for him. Since I was not his girlfriend and barely his friend, instead of a staunch no, I asked him to meet me at the bank the next day.

When he arrived, I promptly announced that I would not be opening the bank account for him, but rather I would help him to open a bank account of his own. He wasn't very thrilled about my announcement. I also encouraged him by saying he was quite capable of managing his personal affairs and didn't need me or anyone else to do it for him.

That day, Dwight opened his very first bank account. He also learned how to complete bank deposits, withdrawal slips, write checks, enroll in online banking, and equally important, to ask banking personnel for assistance when he needed it. Soon afterwards, Dwight obtained his first credit cards and began to discuss investment strategies with his personal banker.

It's funny—I never really set out to make investments in Dwight's life and certainly wasn't expecting anything in return. To me, the support I provided him (teaching, sharing, enlightening, guiding, and supporting) was insignificant and in my mind was the least anyone would offer to a fellow human being to see him or her win at life. For Dwight, he often says it was and remains a lifeline.

As his friend, I was committed to supporting Dwight to achieve the life he envisioned for himself, even if it was only to listen to his plans for the future without judgment or opinion. There were already enough naysayers in his life constantly reminding him of all of the things he could never accomplish because of his past.

A Wife's Superpower

As his wife now, I have supported Dwight in many ways that resulted in his growth and empowerment. However, I don't want to give the impression that I have always been supportive of my husband. That would indeed be misleading. When we were first married, at the advice of a spiritual advisor, I left a sales position earning a six-figure salary to accept a position with a major mortgage lender earning less than forty-thousand dollars per year. We were already under tremendous financial pressure when shortly after our first year of marriage Dwight got laid off from work.

To his credit, Dwight applied for many positions. Due to his felony record, he heard "no" often. The more he heard no, the more apprehensive he became about applying for positions and going on interviews. The less effort I perceived he was making to get back to work to relieve us (me) of our financial burden, the angrier I became. All I knew was he had to get a job because I was NOT going to take care of a man. I would rather be single.

For several months, I resented him for not trying hard enough to save all of the "things" we were losing. I complained often of being tired from working ALL the extra hours necessary to keep us afloat. I constantly reminded him of his failure to provide for us as head of our household. I cried and threw temper tantrums. I withheld sex to punish him. I spoke harshly to him. I literally acted like the warden of our home and treated him like he was a prisoner. The less financial security we had, the more I rebelled in our marriage. The more I rebelled, the less we communicated, and the more I watched my husband recoil.

I was so busy worrying about how our situation affected me, I gave no consideration to what Dwight must have been feeling. Instead I demanded that he go into the world to obtain a job to restore the security I needed.

I never once asked him how it made him feel to lose his job. Was he afraid or disappointed? What specific support did he need from me to help him get back on track? Did he need my encouragement, my praise? How bruised was his confidence in the face of so much rejection? What would help ease his anxiety about having to explain his history to potential employers?

A Wife's Superpower

When I realized that anger and resentment
weren't serving my marriage or me well, I
released those emotions and decided to practice
compassion for my husband instead. We talked,
cried, practiced vulnerability with one another,
and experienced incredible breakthroughs as a
result.

We changed how we managed our finances,
committed to think the best of each other, worked
on our communication skills, and set a mutual
standard of respect for each other as partners in
our marriage.

My greatest learn from that experience happened
the moment I changed my perspective on how I
viewed Dwight. When I saw him as inadequate
and inefficient, that's what he was. When I saw
him as a strong and capable leader in our
marriage, that's what he became.

Instead of continuing in the belief that he was
limited by his past, he made a decision after
attending a "Do It Now!" conference, that despite
his felony record, he wanted to become a licensed
real estate agent. Unbeknownst to me, he also
approached my broker to share his goal and

explain his past. My broker replied, "I think you should go for it."

Armed with the tools he learned in the seminar and the encouragement he received, Dwight asked for my support to help him get his license. At first, I was hesitant. Dwight joined my team as team administrator and did a phenomenal job taking care of our customers. I wanted so badly for that to be enough for him. Everyone loved him, and he loved being a people helper.

I was afraid that his attempt at licensure would only prove disappointing and a waste of time. However, he delivered such a compelling speech as to why he wanted to become a licensee, I became convinced that he should at least make the effort. My only caveat: He would have to do all of the research and the work required to accomplish it.

In the summer of 2017, Dwight enrolled into real estate school and passed. By early fall, we began to compile the mountain of paperwork needed for submission with his application for licensure. By December the application was submitted.

A Wife's Superpower

After six weeks or so, we were notified that his application was pulled by the commission for further review. It was determined that Dwight must appear in person before the commission would make a decision on his request for consideration of licensure.

Right before the initial date to appear, we were advised it was better to hire an attorney familiar with such cases to represent Dwight. Dwight interviewed and selected an attorney. He handled all of the communication and correspondence needed. After thorough review of Dwight's previous case, she agreed to represent him.

When it came time to invest the retainer, I thought to myself, *This is how I'm supporting Dwight... by throwing our hard earned money away?* Dwight believed so strongly that he would be approved for licensure and I knew the importance of remaining supportive of his efforts, so I agreed to invest our resources in Dwight's endeavor.

On May 22, by a vote of four to three, Dwight's request for licensure was granted. It was an emotional and unforgettable day. There were tears, lots of tears. Even people in the audience were moved after hearing Dwight's story. Many congratulated him on the opportunity he received as he walked out of the hearing.

Today, I support my husband by allowing him to be his own person and not trying to prevent him from experiencing disappointment or failure. Before he reached this milestone in his career, I used to think he shouldn't pursue major goals if his past might be a roadblock to him achieving that goal.

By trying to protect him, I only stifled his growth and potential. It's like the caterpillar right before shedding its chrysalis. Even when it appears to be struggling during the process of becoming a butterfly, any intervention in the process will only cripple the caterpillar and cause its subsequent death.

I choose daily to use my Superpower of support to empower my husband to achieve greatness by standing beside him and not in his way, trusting his wisdom and not undermining him, and finally, supporting him with my input as he confidently leads our family in the direction of our highest and best life.

A Wife's Superpower

There's a Chinese proverb that in essence says, "Feed a man a fish, you have to feed him every day. Teach a man to fish and he can feed himself (and others) for a lifetime." Support doesn't always mean doing everything for your husband. Instead, it can mean allowing your husband to do things for himself. Next, you'll read the practical ways I have taught Dwight to "fish" that have benefited him, our marriage, and me.

Here are 3 practical ways you can use Support to naturally and consistently draw the love you need from your husband:

1. Suggest that he tap into his creativity through learning to cook basic meals. While I do enjoy cooking, our schedule doesn't always permit me to cook every day. On nights I would work late, Dwight used to ask me, "What are we going to eat?" I would look at him with disdain thinking, "We are both hungry. I'm still working. Why can't you fix something for us to eat?"

Since Dwight is really good at following step-by-step directions, I created menus for him to learn how to cook simple meals. First it was spaghetti, then vegetables, and later a few meats and beans.

Today he knows how to make several dishes we both enjoy. He makes a mean breakfast too. I no longer create menus for him. In fact, he creates various dishes on his own. If he doesn't know how to prepare something, he accesses YouTube to learn how.

In addition, we now share the responsibility of preparing meals. I still prepare most of the main meals, but the pressure to cook all meals has been removed. Dwight can feed himself when he's hungry and now me too. On the occasion that neither of us has time to fix a meal, we give ourselves permission to eat out or order in.

2. Do not cater to his fears so he discovers how to A.C.T. on his own. Remember when I shared how Dwight wanted me to open a bank account in my name for him? I could have easily enabled him by opening the bank account for him; instead, I taught how him how to A.C.T. (Assess, Choose Courage, and Take Leaps of Faith).

Suggesting that Dwight open his own bank account gave me the opportunity to support him further by teaching him how to complete deposit and withdrawal slips, apply for and obtain credit, speak to account managers, and handle various other types of transactions. Today he manages both our business and personal accounts.

Can you imagine if I had done that? At the time I had no idea we would end up being married. Support can mean helping my husband or doing something for him; however, it most often means allowing him to learn to do things for himself. Had I catered to his fears of not being able to obtain and manage his own bank account then, I might be handling all of our banking business on my own today.

3. Inspire him to lead confidently while being his authentic self. The greatest hurdle I've had to overcome in our marriage was allowing Dwight to fulfill his role as leader in our home. After all, I've always been the breadwinner. I purchased our first home. I started our real estate business, and I have no criminal background therefore I should be the leader, right?

I used to feel since I contributed the most in our marriage that I should have the loudest and final say in everything. In the beginning of our marriage, I admit to emasculating, demeaning, disrespecting, and distrusting my husband although not intentionally. Dwight also believed (and I agreed) that he had no voice (or rights) in our relationship because of his past and his inability to contribute to our life at my same level. I was so wrong.

For years we argued a lot and experienced much pain until I learned how to change my perspective of him, speak encouraging words into his life, praise his accomplishments, show gratitude for his contributions, and honor and respect him for the person he demonstrated himself to be on a daily basis.

I also learned to embrace the idea that I was deserving of having a husband who is a great leader and by no means did I have to settle for less. Sure, Dwight had many hurdles to overcome (me being one of them), but I always knew he was capable of great leadership. He is naturally self-aware, courageous, empathetic, shrewd, strategic, and self-managing. While he made choices that didn't serve him well in the past, who he is authentically speaks to his ability to lead our family today.

When I attempted to lead by myself, I carried all the weight of responsibility; now Dwight and I lead together. I'm the CEO of our real estate business, and he's the CEO of our home.

Personal Notes About Support

_____

_____

_____

_____

_____

_____

_____

_____

_____

_____

_____

_____

_____

_____

_____

_____

_____

_____

_____

_____

_____

_____

_____

_____

_____

_____

About Earitha Anderson

Earitha has a passion for seeing people transcend mediocrity, connect with their purpose, and achieve personal success. She is a quintessential "people helper" who emboldens others to step outside of self-limiting boxes, embrace growth opportunities, and experience their highest and best life. She looks forward to spreading her message through the re-launch of her blog, Back2Basics: Spirit.Soul.Body.

For the past fifteen years, Earitha has expressed her passion for helping through her career as a licensed professional REALTOR®. Together with her husband Dwight, she manages their real estate team, Anderson Real Estate Group, which services Buyers and Sellers in the Jacksonville, Florida, and surrounding areas. Her customers describe her as being passionate, customer-focused, and easy to work with. Earitha's mission is to contribute to the stability of her local community by helping individuals and families achieve the dream of homeownership. She also advocates for those in need of affordable housing, and she endeavors to leave a legacy of service, passion, and results, one sale transaction at a time. Earitha's email contact information is earithaanderson@gmail.com.

Acknowledgments

First, I thank God for empowering me to embrace my authentic self and live my highest and best life.

Dwight, my love, I am grateful for your unconditional love, acceptance, and encouragement to pursue my dreams beyond all perceived limitations.

Mom and Dad, thank you for your example, guidance, and influence to leave this world better than I found it. I hope I make you proud.

Faith, thanks for providing me the space to take my "leap" alongside my gifted co-authors.

Finally, to everyone who has ever motivated me towards greatness… I say THANK YOU!

Chapter 10:
Encouragement

Tyra Williams

In sports, players pat one another on the backside all of the time. That touch is considered a show of love and encouragement. A representation of team chemistry. This pat is also seen between opposing teams as a way of communicating maybe you will win next time. In my marriage, we are a team. Sometimes we oppose one another through disagreements, and sometimes we are on the same side of the agreement. No matter what, we show each other love, we have chemistry, and we may not always win, but we keep going. "A pat on the butt" is sometimes all you need to keep going.

There are plenty of times in our 16 years of marriage that we walk by and touch each other, kiss each other, or pat each other. I am sure you have done the same. Sometimes those touches can cause sparks to fly, and sometimes those touches are just small bits of encouragement. This touch is a way of communicating to your spouse.

A Wife's Superpower

When I met my spouse, we spent a lot of time talking about our hopes and dreams. We were young and dreamy eyed. We chose to get behind one another and help each other pursue our dreams. Now, don't think for one second that we accomplished everything we talked about or dreamed about. We continued to help each other and encouraged each other no matter what. We were determined that no matter what happened in life, we would be stronger together. We married for LIFE, not until we got tired of one another. Anything outside of the Three A's—Affairs, Addictions, and Abuse—can be worked out. You see, life happens. Things come up and sometimes we are left wondering, *What in the heck happened?* You can find yourself thinking, *How did we end up here?* And sometimes you look over at your man and think, *What is wrong with him?* I must admit that at times, I have looked over at my man and wanted to smack him upside the head. I have never done that, but the thought has crossed my mind. If I have to abuse my mate, then I am in trouble.

At times, I have found myself so frustrated with life and in my marriage that I wanted to walk away. According to our life plan, my husband should have been on a couple of tour buses, recorded a few CDs, and gone platinum at least once, by now. Every time it seemed like we were getting close to a breakthrough, life happened. Work, ministry, relocating, miscarriages, pregnancy, premature birth, sickness… life just kept happening.

I found myself so frustrated because we just couldn't seem to touch that dream. I started thinking, *What is wrong with him? Why won't he do what I tell him?* And eventually I found myself thinking, *This is not at all what I signed up for!* I realized that my marriage did not look the way I wanted it to. I did not feel like putting forth the energy to motivate him to do something he should want to do. As previously stated, we decided that divorce was not going to be our first line of defense when things went sideways. (Divorce really is an option, but we make a conscious choice to stay together.) I had to realize that we make plans, but we have to leave room for life. I have learned a few things that I hope will help you too.

1. My husband is a grown man. He is an individual, with his own opinions and thoughts. He thinks the way he thinks, which

A Wife's Superpower

is not the way I think most of the time and there is nothing wrong with that.
2. I needed to learn a whole lot of patience.
3. I needed to turn the kaleidoscope and look at my marriage in a different way. We may not walk the exact path the way we planned. The goal is to keep walking and arrive at our destination with the team healthy and intact.
4. I have the POWER I need to *influence* my spouse, not manipulate him. I had to learn to ENCOURAGE him.

Encouragement[9] is defined as the action of giving someone support, confidence, or hope.

Other words or phrases that describe encouragement are:
- persuasion to do or continue doing something
- inspiration
- motivation
- stimulation
- fortification

As a wife, I find myself often being a source of encouragement. This is just a part of my construct. I have identified this as one of my Superpowers. So, ladies, I want to encourage you all in a couple of areas. As long as we are living,

159

there is potential for good days, bad days, sad days, and angry days. If you ever find yourself in a position where it looks like life isn't going in the direction you want it to go in, remember that you and your sweetie are a Team. You are on the same team. Sometimes he just needs a pat on the backside.

I can recall one of the most challenging times my husband and I faced. Six months before our lease was up, we considered moving to a new city. There were a number of variables to consider. Job, housing, school for our daughter, which city, which side of the family to live closer to, or should we even move? We went back and forth for some months, and to no avail; we had not made any decisions yet. In my mind, I just wanted him to make a decision and get things rolling. In his mind, he didn't want to make the wrong decision. I found it very hard not to lash out at him or be manipulative. At one point I felt so angry that I cried all the way to work, and that ride was 45 minutes. This decision would affect the team, so I didn't want to use the wrong powers.

In my opinion, things were looking pretty bleak. Around this same time, my father got sick and passed. Now, pain, hurt, and grief were inserted into this situation and things took a turn real fast. I was grieving the passing of my dad, and I was about to be homeless. I started to feel lost, displaced, and invisible. Literally—I felt like a child in a corner, paralyzed and afraid to move.

Somehow, we had told ourselves we had to make perfect decisions. I was determined to treat my husband like the grown man he is. Ladies, this means I allowed him to make the decisions needed to steer our family. No matter how hard it was, I remained patient. I went to a counselor and kept my close friends close. I would call two of my friends to vent, so when I got home I could talk to my husband without giving him the stink eye.

One particular night, I remember talking to a friend about this hard decision. After I was encouraged and thought about what she said, I took a step back and looked at our situation. I went home and was able to present different scenarios and outcomes to him in a calm and respectful way. Then I really used my POWER. I told him how much I loved him and that no matter what, we are on the same team. I told him that if he chose a decision I didn't like, I was still on the team. If he chose a decision I did like, I was still on the team. If he chose something and we realized it didn't work out, I was still on the team. We would keep going and eventually things would work out.

This spoke volumes to my honey. So much so, that within days, he started making plans to move our family forward. Encouragement gave him confidence to know that he didn't have to be perfect. It took GREAT effort on my part to use my Superpower. It is so easy to cuss, fuss, roll your eyes and your head, give the silent treatment, and withhold sex. Yes, I said it. You all know exactly what I am talking about. Where does this behavior get you? What does it accomplish? Absolutely nothing!
And yes! I did cuss, fuss, roll my head, and withhold sex (not for long 'cause I love it). It didn't get me anywhere, and it really doesn't feel good.

Instead of all of that destructive behavior, I found that by giving my man a pep talk, it lifted the stress and pressure off both of us. I could not be selfish and encourage him at the same time. You may be thinking who is going to do this for you. That is a valid thought. I promise you that if you give that man a pep talk, you will find that the stress and pressure lifts off both of you. You cannot be selfish and encourage him at the same time. Ladies, you have to remember that this is YOUR man, so this is YOUR job! There is no one I want to influence my man more than me! So, I got serious about my SUPERPOWER.

When I encourage him to use his gifts and talents, it gives me great pleasure and a sense of pride to watch him go. It's kind of hot too. He doesn't have to be perfect.

I want to leave you with one last thought about encouragement. I love country music, I confess. I am fascinated with the whole country scene. I was thinking that when a cowboy needs to get his horse moving, what does he do? Yes, he smacks it on the ass! Now, I ain't calling anyone's man a horse, but you get my point. Go smack him on the hiney, smile, and wink. That just might press the on button and get him moving.

Here are three practical ways you can use Encouragement to naturally and consistently draw the love you need from your husband.

1. Make love not war. The situation we were in was not an issue between us; it was an issue we had to work out together. The decision to move or not was not a relationship issue. It did not break our trust. We were communicating. When you attack your mate, you are not working towards resolution. You are adding new problems that will have to be addressed and worked out. Instead, fortify that man with a little sexual healing. It is healthy! It will help his ego! I promise you that it is good for the whole team!

2. Make him laugh. Every couple has their own way of comedic relief. We are very silly. When I say something that I know will make him laugh, I can see him relax. I can see the stress disappear. This helps take some of the pressure off of his shoulders. Cracking jokes may not solve your problems, but it helps you relax and encourages you both to remember you are in this together.

3. Compliment him. You can do it! Compliment your spouse. It is okay to do it. What is it that you love about him? What are his best qualities?

A Wife's Superpower

Catch him in the bathroom and tell him what he means to you.

Personal Notes About Encouragement

_____
_____
_____
_____
_____
_____
_____
_____
_____
_____
_____
_____
_____
_____
_____
_____
_____
_____
_____
_____
_____
_____
_____
_____
_____

About Tyra Williams

Tyra Williams is a native of Chicago, Illinois. As a child, Tyra developed a love of cooking by watching her mother cook. She would watch cooking shows on television with notebook and pen in hand to write down the recipes and later recreate what she saw. Tyra has been known to cook something tasty wherever she is, and those who know her well would agree.

As Tyra earned her Bachelor of Arts in political science, she baked and cooked for her friends. She later became a caterer and has created cooking videos teaching others how to create dishes for themselves. Tyra loves to cook and see others enjoy food.

Tyra currently resides in the greater Atlanta area with husband Tim and eight-year-old daughter Hanna. She has been married for 15.5 years. Tyra works as a mortgage loan analyst. She desires to travel and take her thirst for culinary knowledge abroad so she recently become a travel agent, in an effort to broaden her life experience and shorten her bucket list. You can reach Tyra on social media outlets Facebook, Twitter, YouTube, and Instagram at @tyrapcooks and email contact information is tpwill@yahoo.com.

Acknowledgements

I would like to:

Thank God for allowing me to meet and marry my husband. God knew the type of man I needed to love me and help me be the best version of me. Without God, this chapter would be different.

Dedicate this chapter to my dad who taught me what a decent man looked like.

Thank my husband tremendously for allowing me to be me, always being there for me, and giving me the freedom to pursue my dreams. Baby, I love you!

A Wife's Superpower

Thank Faith for the opportunity to share a piece of my life with the world and for believing in me.

Thank my mom for teaching me how to be a woman and a mom. Helen, you are the best!

Thank my family and friends, especially the abnormals (you know who are).

Conclusion

You did it! You've reached the end and invested in your personal development. I believe that when you invest in your personal development, every relationship around you changes. Because you have changed. You can no longer accept mediocrity, not standing up for yourself, not having a voice, not taking care of yourself, settling for less, and the list goes on. There is greatness on the inside of you, my dear. You are a powerful woman. Use your power for good.

Marriage can be hard, but it can also be good. There are peaks and valleys in a marriage. You won't always be in the valleys and you won't always be in the peaks. Don't get discouraged because the tips you just read about can transform and enhance your marriage. Give yourself and your husband patience, time, and permission to grow. You both have pasts that influence how you treat yourself and how you treat each other. I hope this book was practical, empowering, and confirming to you. Take care of yourself and remember that you have the right to live your BEST life!

What's your Superpower? You've had plenty of time to think about it, so let us know! We want to hear your testimonial and review of this book. You can email me directly at info@faithjoynercounseling.com to leave a testimonial and review. Please feel free to reach out to the author who influenced you the most. She would love to hear from you!

~ Faith G. Joyner, LMFT

References

Carr, D., Freedman, V.A., Cornman, J., & Norbert, S. (2014).[1] Happy marriage, happy life? Marital quality and subjective well-being in later life. *Journal of Marriage and Family*. Retrieved from https://onlinelibrary.wiley.com/doi/abs/10.1111/jomf.12133

Woods-Giscombe, C.L. (2010).[2] Superwoman schema: African American women's views on stress, strength, and health. *Qual Health Res*. Retrieved from https://www.ncbi.nlm.nih.gov/pmc/articles/PMC3072704/

Communication (n.d.).[3] *In Merriam-Webster's online dictionary* (11th ed.) Retrieved from http://www.merriam-webster.com/dictionary/communication

Introspection (n.d.).[4] *In Merriam-Webster's online dictionary* (11th ed.) Retrieved from http://www.merriam-webster.com/dictionary/introspection

Vulnerability.[5] Dr. Andra Brosh, "How to Practice Vulnerability for Stronger Relationships." Retrieved from www.healthway.com

Emotional Intelligence.[6] *Improving Emotional Intelligence*. Retrieved from https://www.helpguide.org/articles/mental-health/emotional-intelligence-eq.htm

Resilience.[7] *The Road to Resilience*. Retrieved from http://www.apa.org/helpcenter/road-resilience.aspx

Support (n.d.).[8] Retrieved from www.freedictionary.com/support.

Encouragement (n.d.).[9] *In Merriam-Webster's online dictionary* (11th ed.) Retrieved from http://www.merriam-webster.com/dictionary/encouragement.

Additional Resources

National Domestic Violence Hotline: http://www.thehotline.org/ 800.799.7233

National Sexual Assault Hotline: https://www.rainn.org/ 800.656.4673

National Center on Domestic and Sexual Violence: http://ncdsv.org/

Self-Help Book for Women Leaving Abusive Relationships: *Freeing Yourself Financially* by Kristin K. Paul